Acclaim for Lorraine Voss and

"I highly recommend this book, which comes from someone with a lifetime devotion to remaining awake and vitally alive by continually re-membering our human connection with the great Source of all life. *Becoming Awareness* will be of remarkable assistance to you if you wish to be nourished from the energetic connection with Earth; to keep your creative and supportive link with the wisdom of the universe; and to live in natural harmony with All-That-Is."

—Brooke Medicine Eagle, author of *Buffalo Woman Comes Singing* and *The Last Ghost Dance*

"In the spirit of Carlos Castaneda, Lorraine Voss traces her own revealing journey of discovery through her deep relationship with Mexican Seer Nayeli, who holds up the mirror of the Universe to Lorraine. What is revealed is the incredible image of nothingness, the womb of creation, and the realization for the need to recapitulate the man-made stories that deceive nearly all of humanity. Readers searching for knowledge and freedom from the man-made illusion, in which we are embedded, will find Lorraine's discoveries and reconnection to feminine energy very exciting."

—G. Hanson, author of *Not Impossible!: How our Universe May Exist Inside of a Computer*

BECOMING AWARENESS

EARTH. ENERGY. EVOLUTION.

LORRAINE VOSS

RavenCircle Creations
Sedona, AZ

Library of Congress Control Number: 2015959417

Voss, Lorraine.
    Becoming awareness: earth. energy. evolution.
  / Lorraine Voss. - 1st ed.
    ISBN 978-0-9971130-0-6
    1.   Spirituality. 2. Philosophy. 3. Metaphysics.

Printed in the United States of America

CONTENTS

The Glow of Awareness   1

The Importance of Recapitulation   15

Aligning with Source   29

The Curandero   39

Inorganic Beings and Allies   49

Moving Beyond Illusion   61

The Voice of Seeing   73

Bands of Awareness   83

Habitual Patterns and Thought Forms   93

The Changing Face of the Shaman   105

Merging with the Earth   115

Into the Heart of Darkness   127

Inner Silence   139

Integration   153

The Lineage   163

A Dark Force   175

A New Era   187

Evolution   197

Reconnecting to Feminine Energy   207

A Warrior's Purpose   217

Earth - The Final Recapitulation   225

For El Cuervo

This book is dedicated to the Earth stewards, visionaries, mystics, and seers of the world. Through your own deep connection to the Earth and to Source energy, you share a plethora of amazing earth wisdom and silent knowledge. By embracing the totality of what it means to be human as Spirit beings on this amazing earth walk, you ensure, with humility and compassion, that knowledge, wisdom, and truth is ushered into the future on a sturdy bridge of beauty, preservation, and unified awareness.

AUTHOR'S NOTE

As a teenager, I read a book by Robert Monroe entitled, *Journeys Out of the Body,* only to find that the stuff really worked. I could project myself out of my body! It simultaneously terrified me, and left me hungering for more. I soon found myself embarking upon a path of awareness while utilizing the practices that I'd come across from a number of spiritual, philosophical, and metaphysical writings. My commitment was to connect deeply with the earth while freeing myself from the social conditioning of the dominant paradigm.

My travels through Sonora, Mexico ushered me into a long-term and deep relationship with masters of awareness. They taught me how to connect with the abstract through inner silence as well as insights that I can't even describe. They have a temazcal, similar to a sweat lodge, through which we access silent knowledge. Travels around the U.S. brought me to South Dakota where I met a Native American Elder and respected Medicine Man. He took me under his wing, and for nearly ten years taught me how to connect to the pulse of the Earth through the ancient sweat lodge ceremony of steam and purification. He also taught me about vision quest, sitting in silence upon the earth. These teachings led me to live in balance between the earth and sky.

Over the course of many years, I have come to recognize that the earth and the abstract are not separate things; in fact, there is no such thing as separation. We are all connected. Everything that happens to one thing, happens to all things in the web of life, in this great sea of awareness.

The words warrior and seer are commonly used in both

cultures of my benefactors, so I use them throughout this book to indicate a person who is committed to freedom while maintaining a direct link to Spirit. Though there are many words that can be used to define these roles, these terms seem to be the most suitable for the simple fact that there is a lot of illusion to cut through. As we do, we increase awareness and transcend the stories that prevent us from perceiving energy directly.

Some of the terminology used in this book comes directly from ancient concepts and descriptions used by Toltec seers. Their knowledge about energy, the abstract, and the earth is a vital resource for honing awareness and reclaiming our connection to pure life-force energy as it flows throughout the universe. When we release the distractions of the daily world, we are able to perceive the world directly, in a fresh and new way.

We live in a world that is losing its connection to the Earth, and thus its understanding of the deep relationship and synergistic unity that is vital for our existence on this blue planet. For the benefit of all living beings, the time has come to recognize and recapitulate the patterns of social conditioning. This will greatly energize the shift in consciousness that is already underway so we can reconnect, once again, to the great sea of awareness in a sustainable and evolutionary manner.

This book is a work of creative nonfiction based on the experiences I have had in various locations throughout the U.S. and Mexico. While all of the stories in this book are true, I have changed the names of individuals to ensure anonymity. In some cases I have compressed events as well as merged multiple people into one character so I may share this story in a manner which ensures that the essence of the dialogue is both comprehensive and factual.

BECOMING

AWARENESS

The Glow of Awareness

When you come to understand universal life-force energy at its source, you recognize that you are in an eternal flow of collaboration within the universe. You recognize that you are part of the ever-expanding and passionate creation of brilliance and harmonious union within this material reality.
- Nayeli

I met Nayeli on a warm summer day on a beach in Mexico. Those were carefree days when the coastal towns of Sonora were sleepy little fishing villages that had not yet been infiltrated by countless Americans exercising their right to purchase every last grain of sand that graced the coastline of the Sea of Cortez. The Americans that did travel to those areas at that time predominantly lived from their travel trailers, camped on the beach or had modest cabins that blended in with the local color. Life was laid back, a true escape from the great American dream reality found just mere miles across an invisible line called *la frontera*, the border.

Life was simple there and it amazed me to see that people could have very little and be so happy. Everyone I passed would look directly into my eyes and with a smile say *buenos dias*, or *buenas tardes*, an exchange that meant more than hello, it was like saying I *see* you, I recognize your existence. Brightly colored houses with all kinds of flowering trees and colored bougainvillea graced the yards. In the mornings you could smell the delicious aromas wafting out of the bakeries while people lightly sprayed water on the dirt in their front yards to keep the dust down.

Children ran around with carefree abandon playing, not with big wheels, Barbie jeeps, Tonka pick-ups, and other gigantic plastic toys, but using their imaginations driving "buses" made of egg cartons that carried small stones and twigs as "people." The bicycles that they rode were old and worn and had probably spent more time being repaired than ridden but they were used with glee, each child sharing and taking turns, hour after hour, day after day.

There were small family markets in each *barrio* so neighborhood residents had easy access to walk to and purchase the daily necessities for preparing a meal, cleaning the home, and acquiring the essentials for mere pesos. Family cars were old rust-buckets, many of which had the roofs cut out and the doors removed. You can get more people in that way, some standing up while others sat with arms and legs sticking out of every opening, smiling all the way.

I would drive down often and stay at a friend's cabin or in a small motel that cost me about fifteen dollars a night and included a delicious breakfast. Breakfast was served in an open roofed enclosed courtyard with mosaic pots displaying flowering plants, parrots, both loose and in cages, and beautiful heavy carved wooden furniture. At night there were several restaurants but even more roadside taco stands where you could get three beef or fish tacos or a half of a delicious char-broiled *pollo asado*, chicken with beans, all the fixings, and a beverage for about two dollars. Mariachis strolled the streets or cars with gigantic speakers blaring drove by; music always came from somewhere and it was not unusual to see people dancing in the streets.

After spending a carefree day in town I decided to go to the beach at sunset. Walking along the shoreline I picked up a few of the sand dollars that had washed ashore. It always struck me as so incredibly amazing to find these extremely fragile sea urchin skeletons intact. The sky was aglow with bright orange and yellow and deep bands of rust that were deepening as the sun set lower and lower on the horizon. Once the sun had dipped completely below the horizon the colors merged and it truly became what the old Yaqui Indian, don Juan, referred to as the glow of awareness.

The way that I understood the glow of awareness was, when we live in a state of peace and fluidity, our *emanations*, a flow of energetic filaments or luminous lines of energy, become balanced with the emanations of the Earth or greater still, the universe. When these emanations within us become aligned with the force of emanations outside of us then we truly exist within the flow of eternity. We are in synchronistic motion within its frequency and vibration, in perfect harmony and balance. I sat for hours listening to the gentle lapping of the waves as the sky continued to darken and the stars began to appear.

Still thinking about the glow of awareness, I noticed someone coming towards me from the east, walking on the beach along the shoreline. I had an involuntary feeling of panic. There was no one else on the beach, and I thought of grabbing the couple of things I had with me and fleeing to the safety of the house I was staying in. Spirit filled my thoughts, *relax, everything is okay and there is nothing to fear*. My wildly pounding heart would have indicated otherwise. As they got closer I saw that they were carrying something and thought, what the heck, they have a rifle, it's a psychopath from that horrible movie, *El Mariachi*, that I watched not too long ago, and my panic deepened. Determined to remain in a state of trust, I considered that perhaps this was a test towards making death an advisor.

I had convinced myself by now that a man with a rifle was approaching me and would kill me on the spot in a senseless act of violence. Almost accepting it as my fate, it suddenly seemed that it wasn't a rifle at all; it looked like a long rib from a cholla cactus. Within three feet from me now, in the dark, a woman's voice said "*buenas noches*" but I knew that it was not Spanish or English. Not familiar with the language, it seemed possible that she might be either Seri or Yaqui, one of the Indian people who lived in the area. "Buenas noches," I responded. She stood there for a minute and then said, "May I sit down?" in whatever foreign language she was speaking. Saying yes to her, she sat right next to me, practically shoulder to shoulder facing the sea as I was. She placed the cholla rib on the sand to her right.

What suddenly occurred to me was that she was speaking a language I couldn't even identify, yet I understood her! I spoke to her in Spanish but she was responding in what was gibberish to me, although it was as clear to me as if she had been speaking English. And then we just sat there in silence for what seemed to be a long time.

I became uncomfortable with this silence between two strangers who spoke different languages yet understood each other. I said in Spanish, "It's such a beautiful night, the sea is so serene."

She replied in her language, "Yes, it is beautiful and I'm happy to be sharing this moment with you."

How is it that I can understand her ran through my mind over and over again. This is insane.

And then she laughed lightly and said in perfect English, "Well, well, this is most certainly a sign from the Spirit."

"You speak English!" I accused her.

She laughed harder this time and said yes, "but I also speak the Zapotec language and even though you don't understand it you knew everything I said."

"Who are you? How could this be? What the heck is going on?" My mind was racing with the incredulous nature of the encounter so I continued. "You've scared me half to death, I thought you were a man with a rifle about to kill me right here on the beach. Where did you come from? Are you real or is this some kind of strange dream?"

She assured me that this was very real and also a dream, but that there was nothing peculiar about it.

"What does that mean, very real and also a dream? It's either real or it's a dream so which is it?" I demanded to know.

She laughed again and said nothing. I looked at her, and though it was pretty dark out, I saw that she had long black hair falling loosely to the middle of her back. She was barefoot and wore a skirt and a sleeveless blouse. I could see some silver earrings dangling in the little light that reflected on us from the stars and crescent moon.

"Now from what I gather," she said matter-of-factly, "you have been sitting here contemplating the glow of awareness and yet you question the possibility of being in dream. That's a bit incongruous, don't you think?"

"Yes, as a matter of fact I have been contemplating the glow of awareness, but how can you possibly know that, are you a witch?" I asked her.

She laughed again and said that she preferred to think of herself as a seer and that from very far down the beach she saw a luminescence and walked down to see what it was where upon she discovered me.

"Really?" I asked, "I was glowing?"

"Yes, and you were so intriguing I just had to investigate. And I'm glad I did. Had I not heeded the call of the Spirit, we both would have missed this extraordinary opportunity. My name is Nayeli, by the way. And you, my dear, are a *vidente*, a seer," she added.

I have always known myself to be intuitive but had never considered myself a seer. I liked her a lot; she was very direct, authentic and enigmatic while being joyful and radiant.

"Were you sent here to be my teacher?" I asked. It was actually not as far-fetched of a question as it might seem. I had started to re-read the books of Carlos Castaneda and intended a teacher to help me make sense of everything. When I noticed someone coming towards me, I had actually been thinking about the glow of awareness and what don Juan talks about in Castaneda's book *The Fire from Within*. He discusses the mastery of awareness with three sets of techniques and I had hoped, just before Nayeli approached me, for a teacher who could help me to learn.

In response to my question about her being my teacher she said, "There is nothing I can teach you; however, I can help you to forget many things so you may find clarity and remember what's important."

We talked for hours on that beach, late into the early morning. Nayeli provided me with a very brief personal history explaining to me that she was raised in both Mexico and the US, the daughter of a Zapotec Indian man and an American woman. Thus, she spoke three languages fluently; Spanish, the Zapotecan language, and English. The Zapotec Indians, she clarified for me, are one of the oldest Mesoamerican cultures with the belief that their people did not migrate to Oaxaca, but instead, had descended from the Clouds and became known as the Cloud People, a myth she enjoyed immensely.

As the horizon started to lighten in the east I yawned sleepily and she said, "This has certainly been delightful but I must be going now, I really need to get some sleep and it seems that you do too."

"When will I see you again?" I asked. She told me to meet her at the taco stand that the locals refer to as *el ferrocarril,* the train station, the next evening at six o'clock.

As I walked back to the house, I couldn't even imagine how I would be able to sleep; I had so many questions, so much information to sort through. As I lay in bed, I gave thanks for the good fortune I had that day and looked forward to seeing Nayeli again.

I met Nayeli at el ferrocarril at 6:00 p.m. as we had planned. We each sat on a folding chair at a square and rickety aluminum table that had a Corona Extra logo on it. I began to tell her about a most unusual dream I had the night before, just as our tacos and beverages were brought to our table. She looked amused and asked me to tell her about my dream.

"It was very different from other dreams I have had. It felt very lucid and real, as though it wasn't a dream at all. It started with me walking through a very humid and dense jungle which made me hot and sweaty. I have never been in the jungle before, but knew it was a jungle, in fact, one that was very familiar to me. Following what sounded like birdcalls echoing nearby led me in a direction that put me on a well beaten path that seemed familiar too. I came upon a large clearing in the trees with what appeared to be a water hole filled with crystal clear turquoise blue water. I have never seen anything like it, so beautiful and pristine. And yet, it wasn't the first time I had seen it.

"There were small fish swimming in in the water. Kneeling at the edge I put my hand in the water and found it to be cool and refreshing. Tasting a drop allowed me to determine that it was fresh and not salt water. I stood up, jumped in, and floated there for a long time feeling cleansed, renewed, and refreshed. It didn't occur to me how exhausted I was until I got out. Sleep came fast at the edge of the pool and when I awoke it was nighttime. An immensity of brilliant stars filled the sky with the full moon rising. A mass moved through the sky to right above where I sat. It began to spin slowly and took the form of a spiraling cloud. It was mesmerizing."

I inhaled deeply then exhaled hoping to reconnect to the dream so the full experience could be accurately conveyed.

"After a while the spiraling cloud took the form of a whirlwind and the bottom part of the funnel was moving down towards the Earth right above me. In short time the whirlwind consumed me and I began to spiral slowly within it. Rising within the whirlwind it resumed the form of a cloud and then began to take on the shape of a serpent. I sat on its back as it moved across the sky, looking down at the jungle that was illuminated by the full moon. And then I awoke."

"Fascinating," said Nayeli as she spooned some hot sauce onto her taco. "Are you familiar with Toltec history?" she asked.

"No, not the history but I have read Carlos Castaneda's books if that counts," I said.

"Hmmm, our meeting is becoming more and more auspicious," she stated.

"Why is that and what about the Toltec?" I asked.

"Suffice it to say there are no accidents. The Toltec are men and women of knowledge, masters of awareness. They are ancient seers who have a deep understanding of abstract knowledge that has been passed down to them from a benefactor. They have discovered from sitting in silence that there is unfathomable knowledge and energy available to them independent of language and tangible information. They constantly challenge themselves to evolve beyond the realm of ordinary human awareness and are dedicated to learning anything that they can in order to consistently gain access to the power we all have when we are aligned with Source energy."

After processing some of what was new information to me, I asked: "Are you a Toltec, Nayeli?"

"I am a warrior who is committed to aligning with the abstract, constantly striving to increase my energy in order to access knowledge and total freedom. Since this has been the life work of Toltec people then I suppose I can be perceived as a Toltec." Nayeli's smile was both modest and comforting.

"Are Toltec people a race or can anyone be a Toltec?" I asked, very curious to learn more.

"More than being a specific race, being Toltec is a philosophy, a way of life. The ancient Toltec were people strongly dedicated to learning all they could about the Earth and the cosmos, to heighten their awareness and to perceive beyond the boundaries of human limitation that they've been taught. They were particularly interested in the fact that the entire universe and everything within it is part of one single and complex energy system. If one is committed to awareness and is dedicated to total freedom, then they may be considered a Toltec." Again she smiled. "It's just a label though, a definition that can apply to so many people whether they have an understanding of Toltec culture or not. It's a big subject, and I want to get back to our previous conversation. Do you understand what the dream you told me about means?" she asked me.

"Well no, not at all," I replied. "I hoped that you would be able to offer some insight," I told her, truly hoping to understand what this strange dream represented.

"Let's begin with the water hole you saw. From what you describe, it is a cenote. A cenote is part of an intense, underground cave system that is linked to sinkholes like the one that you swam in in your dream. The largest system of this type of underground caves is on Mexico's Yucatan peninsula, surrounded by jungle. These cenotes provide fresh water to the Mayans and are considered sacred. Besides being a water source, the Mayans believe that the cenotes are portals imbued with sacred power that lead to other worlds."

Impressed with her knowledge I slowly digested what

Nayeli was telling me.

"The part about the spiraling cloud is quite amazing. According to Mesoamerican legend, the first leader of the Toltec was named Mixcoatl. The name comes from two Nahuatl words; *mixtli* which means cloud and *coatl* which means serpent. The word coatl, however, can also be interpreted as twin. Mixcoatle is more commonly known as a cloud serpent although there is another interpretation. The Nahuatl language was spoken among the Toltec, Aztec and Nahua peoples. To them, Mixcoatle can also be interpreted as a double being, a being that resides in both worlds, simultaneously on Earth and in the cosmos. As a double being it is said that Mixcoatle symbolizes both the masculine and feminine as an embodiment of its creation and becomes the bridge that moves between Earth and sky."

I had so much to absorb. "That sounds really profound Nayeli. I'm not sure I even understand what it means," I said trying to comprehend the totality of her explanation. "Why did I have this dream? What does it mean to me?" I asked. "What does this dream mean for me?"

"It certainly is a strong omen. I typically don't interpret other people's dreams for them since I feel that dreams are of a personal nature and should be interpreted by the person who has them. Since you have a limited understanding of the Toltec history, I'd like to offer an explanation if you are willing and open to receive it," she said.

"Yes, of course! I would appreciate an explanation. It was such a vivid dream, and I am very much interested in knowing as much as I can about it," I said to her.

"Remember that what I am offering you comes from my

perspective and may take on different meaning for you. I do not, by any means, want to fixate the position of your *assemblage point*, only offer my two cents so that you may further reflect on this dream. Do you know what the assemblage point is?" she asked.

I nodded affirmatively and replied eagerly. "The assemblage point, as I understand it, is a vortex or epicenter of energy located near the center of our breastbone. It is here at this point where our perceptions of the reality that we each maintain is assembled. We have the ability to allow our assemblage points to remain fluid so we can live in the moment without having attachments to anything. On the other hand, we are capable of having the position of our assemblage point become fixated upon a story which can solidify a thought form or idea within us."

Nayeli's nod encouraged me to continue. "In either case," I said, "the energy of the assemblage point can be shifted from a fixated position in order to become fluid or, it can be shifted from a fluid position to become fixated. Words, it turns out, have the potential to fixate the position of one's assemblage point.

"Exactly," she said. "That was well said and I'm glad that you understand this. You and I met on the beach yesterday. You expressed to me that you are seeking a teacher to assist you on your own path which is, from the sound of it, aligned with the ancient Toltec as described by the books you have read by Carlos Castaneda. The dream you had is strongly connected to the understanding I have of the culture of my father's people.

"First," she said, "nothing happens by accident. The cloud that you witnessed moving across the sky encompassed you in a spiral. A spiral spins around and around in a circle, each time in a new way without ever repeating itself. The spiral is reflected in the natural world and throughout the universe. We even live in a spiral galaxy. It represents the constantly flowing universal energy of growth and evolution: always seeing everything through new eyes while being open to change and new awareness. Does this makes sense to you?" she asked.

"Yes," I replied excitedly. "I am deeply committed to increasing my awareness, to releasing the patterns that bind me to the so-called group mind in order to advance towards total freedom. It all makes so much sense!" I exclaimed marveling over my good fortune to having met this extraordinary women.

"Good," she said, and I could tell by looking at her that the gears in her head were turning as she replayed my dream in her mind. "What interests me most about Mixcoatle appearing to you is not in the common interpretation of the cloud serpent. What interests me most," she repeated, "is the less commonly known aspect of Mixcoatle representing a double being as a bridge between the Earth and the sky. The Spirit has something in store for you. Very intriguing indeed."

"Why, Nayeli, what does it mean?" I implored. I was confused once again.

"All I can say is that everything happens for a reason, and I would be honored to assist you in your journey of discovery; to assist you in connecting to the universal life-force energy that holds everything in gentle balance and in freedom. But in order to do this, you must agree that our relationship will not be as teacher to student; we will be equals on a parallel journey. As I said, there is nothing I can teach, I can only guide you and hold a mirror in front of you so that you may see your own reflection within it." Nayeli smiled a peaceful smile.

I did not know exactly what she meant and didn't feel as though her explanation of my dream brought me any more clarity. But I already knew in my heart that she was going to be the most influential and powerful teacher I would ever know so I just nodded, smiled back, and said in a barely audible whisper, "Okay."

The Importance of Recapitulation

We have tons of energy, we are pure energy. If we choose to recall and revisit past occurrences, we are simply feeding them which ultimately makes those past occurrences stronger and more prevalent. Who wants to hold on to old energy? To do so weakens and prevents us from being in the moment within the continual evolutionary act of creation or co-creation. You must recapitulate.
- Nayeli

Early one morning in late June, Nayeli and I left her house to wander through the Sonoran Desert and harvest the luscious fruit of the saguaro cactus. The Sonoran Desert is the only place in the world where saguaros grow, and we are so fortunate and grateful to have access to this delicious fruit. We wore strong, sturdy hiking boots to maneuver through the desert brambles, prickly pear cactus, and the rocky arroyos. We each carried a citrus fruit picker, a pole that had a large wicker basket at the end. These pickers enabled us to reach up about twelve feet to retrieve the fruits of our labor. It also served as a staff to help us keep our balance through the arroyos, and as Nayeli said instilling a bit of fear, a tool with which to flick away any rattlesnakes we encountered.

We left at four-thirty in the morning to ensure that we would return home no later than nine a.m. since the summer heat is so harsh while enduring any amount of activity. Before we began to collect the fruit, Nayeli took out a small packet of bee pollen and left some as an offering at the base of the first saguaro we encountered that bore fruit. She said a simple statement of gratitude for this gift from the Earth.

As we began to harvest the beautiful bright red fruits, Nayeli talked about the necessity of reclaiming the energy that was taken from me as well as that which I had squandered, relinquished willingly, or disbursed throughout my lifetime. She explained that reclaiming energy is a process through which we essentially recapture all of the energies we expended in the past. This restoration includes interactions with people and any emotions, good, bad or neutral, that arise throughout our lives. She said this is best accomplished when we start in the present and then follow our memories back to the earliest time that we could remember.

"How is it possible to follow our memories all the way back to the beginning of our life?" I asked, feeling a bit daunted by such a momentous task.

"When we start to reclaim our energy it is restored and as a result we increase our current energetic structure. As we continue this important process, we gain more and more energy. Over time, we restore our life-force energy to its original whole and complete configuration through which we became manifest in human form," she said matter-of-factly.

"Reclaiming energy works when we completely release the thought forms that keep us bound to specific incidences in our lives. These cause us to become trapped within a vicious cycle of replaying repetitive and draining emotional conflict. The continual rehashing of patterns causes our life-force energy to be constantly wasted."

"So what you're saying, Nayeli, is that the energy that we

have expended in various situations throughout our lives may cause us to perpetuate old stories?"

"Exactly," she said as she placed several saguaro fruits into her basket. "People have a strong tendency to remain fixated upon certain stories and events that already occurred in their lives. This even applies to pleasurable and gratifying experiences that they attempt to experience again and again only to find that they are unable to recreate the event. Their energy became trapped in the original experience, and they find themselves attached to a specific outcome. Unable to repeat the situation with the profundity they experienced the first time it occurred leaves them feeling unfulfilled and emotionally drained."

I thought about events in my own life that I had tried to recreate for the simple fact that they were so enjoyable, and how repetitive attempts to relive them always seemed to leave me feeling dissatisfied and even irritable.

"We have tons of energy, we are pure energy," Nayeli said excitedly. "The practice of reclaiming energy means to take back and recover lost energy. And it's easy! All we have to do is start by taking some time out of our day with clear intention of essentially reclaiming our power. As we reclaim power we free up the energy that makes it possible for us to see more examples of where or to whom we lost energy and then we just keep recapitulating.

"To avoid this practice prevents us from freeing ourselves of these old energies and personal stories. This can cause our bodies to have energetic blockages which may eventually lead to depression, anxiety, fear, sadness, illness and disease. On the other hand, to free ourselves from these old energies enables us to have excess power, which allows for creativity to flow easily. This fluidity provides us with feelings of well-being and increased awareness."

Nayeli was intent on reaching a bunch of cactus fruit on a very tall saguaro. When she grasped them with her picker she said, "Many years ago, when I started this practice, I would sit quietly outdoors and energetically connect with the winds. The wind comes from all directions and blows away the things that no longer serve us. Since the wind has the potential to shift the position of our assemblage point, it also assists in reminding us of events to recapitulate. I would begin by thinking about recent people I had interacted with or situations that I had experienced. Remember, it's all energy and the focus needs to be placed on reclaiming power.

"In short time a situation would emerge to which I had lost energy. The energy that I reclaimed was all of it, negative energy, positive energy, sexual energy, all energy. As people and situations revealed themselves to me, I would breathe deeply into myself the energy that had been expended in those situations, and through the exhalation I would release those recollections of the past. In so doing I gained more energy which allowed other past situations to easily present themselves. The practice eventually became easy to do in the moment."

"Did you perform arm sweeps or turn your head from side to side?" I asked recalling some techniques I had read in a book.

"No, I did not. Motions of that sort are not necessary once you have set your intention. The key to success lies in the breath. You may feel like moving your head or arms or hands as emphasis to your practice but the breath is the power behind the intention."

"So," I began as I thought of all she had told me to this point, "how do you recapitulate in the moment?"

"You remain aware of your energy at all times. If a

situation arises where you feel as though you may lose energy, you connect with the breath and allow the moment to pass through you. In so doing you become impeccable with your energy and will avoid wasting it on anyone or anything."

"How do you erase all of those memories from your mind?" I asked.

"You are not erasing them from your mind and you are not denying that they existed. What you are doing is returning to your own vital and essential life-force energy that you were born with but have given away throughout the years. You must pull back all of your energy into the center of your being to become unattached from the situations to which you had expended the energy in order to be free. Think of it as cleaning your links to power. It is a matter of restoration and renewal.

"If you continue to revisit the negative situations in your life or worse, share your stories of pain with others over and over again, you wind up feeding the past and giving it more energy. If you give your life-force energy to past traumas that you are trying to release, they will become so big that they may consume you."

I took a big swig of water from my water bottle. It was starting to get really hot already. Nayeli noticed me and reminded me to conserve my water because we had a couple of hours to go and it was going to get hotter.

"How do you wind up giving the past more energy if you share those stories?" I asked hoping she wouldn't tire of my incessant questioning.

Nayeli stopped and put her picker down and took a small sip of her own water. She sat down on a rock, so I took that as a sign that we were going to rest for a while and sat down on the ground near her. "When someone fails to reclaim energy that had been lost to an event," she said, "the energy that remains linked to that past event has the potential to become energized as the story is retold. They wind up energizing the emotions that had arisen at that time. As a result, the storyteller comes to feel empowered through the rehashing of the story and unwittingly lives in the past.

"I'll give you an example," she said. "I met a woman years ago who repeatedly asked me to go out for a coffee with her. I declined over and over again because I could see a deeply ingrained story in her life that consumed her; one that she wanted to feed. I bumped into her at the house of a mutual friend and she all but begged me to meet with her and I finally acquiesced. We met at a coffee shop and from the moment we sat down she divulged the discord of her life, complete with horrid tales of physical, emotional, and sexual abuse. At some point I stopped listening to her words and was watching her energy body expand as she became more and more animated, emphasizing certain points in her story, particularly the most horrible ones, trying ever so diligently to get some kind of rise out of me.

"It became apparent that she was no longer harboring pain from these events and instead, had come to rely upon the reaction of others to energize her. I sat and endured her story with a vacant look upon my face for two solid hours without so much as a peep. When she realized that she was not getting the response that had fed her for all those years long after the actual incidents had occurred, she slumped back in her chair. With a confused look of exasperation, she exclaimed, 'Wow. You're the first person that I've told this story to who hasn't had some kind of reaction or comment!'"

"I kept silent for about a minute or so while watching as

her energy body, which had anticipated some of my energy as sustenance, begin to deflate and she sank further back into her chair. I finally said, 'You can continue telling this story to others so that you can become energized through another person's shock, compassion, or pity. This choice will keep you as a victim to your story, a slave to your past. Or,' I continued, 'you can make the choice to reclaim your power from those situations so that you can become free and energized in new and creative ways.'"

"What did she say, Nayeli, did she make a choice?" I asked with anticipation.

"She thanked me for meeting with her, and said that she had to leave to go and pick-up her son from school," said Nayeli.

"And that was that?" I asked, disappointed to have not some kind of finale to the example Nayeli provided to me.

Nayeli laughed at the look of exasperation on my face and said, "I would not have been surprised if I never saw her again, but I did run into her one day after about a year and while she looked the same, her energy had shifted considerably. She said, 'Thank you so much for not energizing my story that day when we met for coffee'. She went on to tell me how she had made the choice to release the story, reclaim her power, and that her life couldn't be better. In fact, she was helping others to do the same."

"That's wonderful, Nayeli!," I said as the two of us got up and began to move towards some saguaros that were loaded with fruit.

"In addition to reclaiming and restoring life-force energy within ourselves, it is of utmost importance," she said, "to remain mindful that we are not falling back into the stories and patterns that we have been taught to perceive. Once we liberate ourselves from our childhood and young adult conditioning, we must make it a point to take a closer look at our foundational make-up. This helps us to arrive at the realization that we no longer need to uphold certain traits and characteristics that were taught to us. We can begin to recreate ourselves by embodying the things we felt deprived of while we were forced to fit within the patterns of humanity that were imposed upon us.

"At this point we become excited with the possibility of recreating ourselves, and we fully immerse ourselves into new roles by learning everything there is to know about becoming ourselves. This can liberate us or entangle us in another pattern. If we wind up obsessed with our new role, we come to realize that our assemblage point has, once again, become fixated, this time, by our own doing. It is at this juncture that one decides whether to find solace in the security of her routines or to continue jumping into the abyss. The warrior jumps," she said boldly.

"The only thing that prevents us from evolving into states of consistent, heightened awareness and transcendence of human limitations is ourselves. It is so easy to consistently fall back into the stories and patterns that we have been taught to perceive. The force behind collective coercion is so strong, so reasonable, and so unified. Its hold on us places us at the center of everything which makes us feel important. The more important we feel, the more difficult it becomes to evolve.

"What motivates me on this path is the constant beauty, mystery and awe unraveling before me." Nayeli's eyes shone with conviction and she continued. "I know that when I allow my assemblage point to become fixated, everything becomes tedious and I can feel myself solidifying. This density is the reminder I need to remain determined enough to constantly strive for fluidity. I recapitulate often and align with creation in every moment."

I watched her with a sense of wonder, mesmerized by her knowledge and the ease with which she explained it. "You should be so proud of yourself, Nayeli. You have accomplished feats that most people cannot even comprehend," I said, proud of myself for even knowing her.

"I also recognize," she quipped, "that when I become full of myself by thinking that my dedication to this path has really paid off and provided me with more awareness, just how full of beans I am. Then, I recapitulate the awareness I think I hold, so that I can lose that bit of self-importance. I hold on to nothing and become empty again. When we can admit that we know nothing is when we are able to perceive the fullness of creation. Then we come to realize how very little we actually know. The only thing left to do is to seek to know something new in the never-ending and fulfilling battle for awareness. And this is the ultimate gift, to keep dancing the dance of emptiness, of fluidity, of eternal evolution!"

We moved towards another area and startled a desert hare. We both laughed as the blur of gray fur darted from place to place trying to escape our intrusion.

"What you need to remember, Lorraine, is that everything is energy. Women typically move energy out from their center as a way to take care of people or as a way to keep peace in their environment. As a warrior, recapitulation allows us to reverse that outpouring of energy so that we may bring it back into our center. We are renewed with powerful life-force energy as the result of changing the direction of the wind, the wind that resides within us. As a result we recognize that we will never lose energy to people, events or situations again. With humility and resolve we remain centered in our own inner power, immovable and steady."

Just as Nayeli finished her thought, a wind blew towards us from the North, hot and steady. "Open all your senses and breathe this wind in through your center," Nayeli shouted, startling me. "Listen to what it has to teach you!"

I closed my eyes and lifted my face to the oncoming wind. It blew my hair as my face was lightly struck with tiny bits of sand and debris. The sound of the desert wind rushed past my ears and inside my body. In fact, I noticed, there were no other sounds, only that of the wind. I drew my breath deeply into the center of my being.

At first I thought it was Nayeli, but then I realized it was the wind speaking to me. As I listened, I heard that every thought has the potential to become a reality. If it is a positive thought, there exists the possibility for it to manifest in our life. Likewise, if it is a negative thought then it, too, has the potential to manifest. Each and every thought becomes a thought form out there in the wind, feeding off of our energy, waiting for us to continue to feed it, shape it, create it into becoming the thing it was intended to be. These thoughts need to be recapitulated. All thoughts need to be recapitulated. Thoughts of the future need to be recapitulated!

I felt the wind subsiding and opened my eyes. I saw Nayeli looking past me, out into the distance. I turned around and saw a *dust devil*, a plume of dust, like a miniature tornado, rising behind me. It carried small sticks, an errant plastic bag, and dust along with it. It whirled and whirled, rising higher into the clear blue sky, then it dissipated completely, and we were sitting in total silence. Total stillness.

Nayeli and I looked at each other with complete surprise. She said, "Well, that was an auspicious sign if I ever saw one!"

"What did it mean, Nayeli?" I asked.

"For one, the wind came in and from the looks of it, delivered a message to you. What did you sense or receive from it?" she asked.

"Wow, that was intense!" I exclaimed. "At first I thought you began to talk to me but then I realized that I did receive a message from the wind." I paused trying to reconnect to the energy of the event and to find the words so I could relay them to Nayeli.

"The wind told me that every thought has to be recapitulated because all of our thoughts, positive and negative, are awaiting the necessary energy in order to manifest. It's as if they are lingering out there in the universe waiting to be sculpted, nurtured, and created into form. There seemed to be an urgency in the wind to recapitulate all thoughts including thoughts of the future. Does any of this make sense to you, Nayeli?"

"Yes, it most certainly does. What else did you notice about the wind?" she asked.

"I remember getting hit in the face with little bits of debris and sand. Oh, I just remembered. All sounds except for that of the wind went away, and I heard the wind blowing simultaneously around me and inside of me," I exclaimed.

"The dancer on the wind visited you," Nayeli said while looking at me and through me. "The dancer on the wind is a powerful omen indeed, especially when she dances in from the north. She ushers in the life-force awareness that assists you in remembering the eternal awareness from which you arrived. She is symbolic of change and blows away the chaos and misperceptions that fill the mind. She brings clarity and reminds us that we are universal beings.

"More interesting is that she left in a whirlwind, like the spiral spinning around and around to the same point without ever repeating itself." Nayeli added, "The very pinnacle of what it means to recapitulate."

It was hard to tell who was more excited, me or Nayeli.

"What's so interesting to me," I began, "is that the voice of the wind said that thoughts become form and to recapitulate the future. I mean, if every single thought out there becomes energized by the creator of the thought and multitudes of others who feed that thought form, then it is bound to become a reality, is it not?"

"That's why we have to be so careful with our thoughts and our actions," Nayeli said. "When we create a thought, it has the potential to take form and is why we are able to manifest into our lives. Our thoughts become our creation, and this can be a very positive thing when you consider that we are the creators of our reality and have the power, when aligned with universal energy, to attract and produce well-being and beauty in our lives."

Nayeli continued, "Positive thoughts have to leave the mind so they can merge with intent in order to become manifest. We cannot have any attachment to those thoughts or else they become weighted with expectation." Only after a few moments when she seemed certain that I understood, she continued. "When a negative thought arises, we must be certain to eradicate that thought immediately, to strike it from our minds. If we do not, the negative thought becomes a parasite that will feed off of us in anticipation of its full creation. And if we do wind up feeding that negativity and ultimately create it, when others become aware of its existence, they will either refuse it or accept it. If it is accepted, it will gain more power, a life of its own and may have the capacity to hurt, alter, or destroy."

With our bags filled with cactus fruit and the temperature rapidly rising, we decided to head back to the house. We were quiet on our return trip; dusty, weary, hot, each lost in our own thoughts. Recapitulate the future, I thought: of course! If we plan or prepare for any outcome, then we are losing energy to the outcome by envisioning how it might be. And if it arrives differently from what we envisioned, we may miss it completely. What we need to do is align with Source. Right here, right now. When we align with Source with fluidity, we dance along the lines of awareness that are unfolding in the moment.

We cannot be warriors of freedom when thoughts of freedom fixate the position of our assemblage point. We amass power and energy when we recapitulate the past. We amass power and energy when we recapitulate the future. When we do this we are able to live without distractions and in total freedom for the simple fact that we are already free. We return to being the creative force that we were born to be when we sit within silent knowledge, completely aligned with intent. Thank you, dancer on the wind. I have my work cut out for me.

Aligning with Source

When people align with intent, they are looking into and feeling the unknown. They are connected to the very fabric of existence and become one with the energetic fibers of the universe, flowing freely in the current of creation.

- Nayeli

The day was as still and hot as are most summer days in the desert. The cicadas were buzzing loudly as I sat on a high rock out-cropping that had come to be called *punto intento*, or place of intent, by the small group of seers Nayeli knew and whom I now spent some time with. This vantage point provided a 360 degree view of the pulsating, lush, and often harsh Sonoran desert. Looking out over a sea of saguaro, prickly pear, cholla, and organ pipe cactus along with ocotillo, mesquite and palo verde trees, I watched the energy of the desert vibrate above the landscape.

I got the hang of recapitulating and felt energized and renewed. I now contemplated the new task Nayeli gave me to stalk awareness while ceaselessly recapitulating the patterns, or the man-made stories, that are maintained in the dominant social paradigm. This social disorder consists mostly of living in compliance within a system that claims to have absolute power over everyone and everything. Nayeli had agreed vehemently with what I already believed, that humans view themselves to be superior over all other species and will stop at nothing to consume the Earth's resources with little regard to the Earth or the other beings that live upon her.

The previous evening Nayeli explained to me that in order to successfully accomplish my task I had to connect even more deeply with the lines of awareness from a feminine perspective. It was time, she explained, for me to move my assemblage point completely from its fixated position of everything I thought I knew. This would help me to evolve beyond the acceptable goals and subtle limitations that are inherent in most areas of life, including education, career, relationships, attitude, emotions, and spiritual belief systems.

"The teachings from the books you read are sometimes essential in arriving at the bridge between the worlds but not necessary once one has become aligned with pure conscious awareness. This," she continued, "is universal life-force energy, the primordial energy of all that is which flows through and around us at all times. Some people refer to this energy as the Spirit, the divine, intent, or God. However, the words and descriptions offered through myths and stories often create definitive descriptions that limit our ability to perceive with clarity."

To simplify our conversations, we agreed to refer to this energy as *Source*, which allows one to be connected to raw energy as it flows, without becoming fixated upon a specific concept.

"The real work," she emphasized, "is in the walk and the practice. There are areas that men must focus on just as there are areas that women must focus on in order to arrive in wholeness and balance at the threshold of total freedom.

"Feminine energy is raw power, a graceful dance of beauty

upon the Earth and through the cosmos. One of the things that separate the female seer from the male seer is her ability to connect to dozens of lines of awareness simultaneously if she is willing to open to silence. While men typically grab onto a single line and follow it to its end with precision, accuracy, and incredibly focused intent, women can effortlessly travel along multiple lines while holding each point of awareness congruently, allowing her to take in much broader perceptual awareness at once. This in turn allows her to fit the pieces of the puzzle of humanity together effortlessly amidst the chaotic stories that have been told upon this Earth for thousands of years."

It was true, I thought, as I watched a jack-rabbit dart through the desert. Little is said about the power of feminine energy which has the potential to dream awake a new dream here on Earth. Women who are committed to the seers path are able to systematically destroy the outmoded energetic lines that support and maintain our current paradigm.

Through Nayeli I had learned that every point in time, every word, every action, has the ability to influence a progression that can be both beneficial and detrimental. When we warriors of freedom recapitulate our personal stories and become fluid enough to recapitulate in the moment, we acquire the energy that is necessary to move into *second attention*, a realm of pure perception. This comes as a result of the massive amount of personal energy we are able to restore through the disciplined practice of recapitulation. From here, in second attention, the man-made stories that cocoon the Earth begin to reveal themselves and a seer finds herself recapitulating those stories.

We discover that most of those stories have become patterns that were created by others and have not been recapitulated. As a result of all these floating stories, a false energetic man-made matrix encircles the Earth in which other stories continue to become enmeshed. This dilutes the pure universal life-force or Source energy that ushers in cohesion, balance, and true wisdom.

The way to approach my task was becoming clearer to me as I spent time away from the distractions of the world. Increasing awareness occurs naturally when we remove ourselves from the bombardment of external stimuli. Without the constant assault on our senses, we are able to discover the origination point behind the nature of existence and why it exists the way it does. We come to witness pure energy as it emerges from the place of pure intent.

Recapitulating the patterns of humanity, however, sounds a little daunting, and yet, based on what Nayeli shared with me, I came to realize that recapitulating these man-made stories would be best accomplished if I could do the work with a male warrior. It would involve mutual and balanced seeing.

Nayeli once told me that when a woman comes to understand how the energetic lines became entangled and intertwined by so many stories, she can, from a place of silence and intention, dance within them all, unravel them, recapitulate them and move ever so gracefully into freedom from them. At times, an energetic line to a story will surface that was created by a man, perhaps thousands of years ago, that cannot be fully comprehended. Through shared seeing, a male seer has the ability to "ride" the line back to its inception with focused intent that burns into the moment it was created. He brings that point of knowledge into the present with clarity and precision. We are then able to unwrite it from the fabric of existence. Together, we energetically disentangle it from other stories and belief structures that have energized that story and given it power from the time it was created.

I worked hard to understand everything she told me but did not yet have the experience of doing this kind of work in balance with a man. I reflected on another part of the conversation with Naeyli, and wondered how to best incorporate her information into my work with a male seer.

"With knowledge and awareness," she told me, "the female seers that I know, engage in a beautiful dance that we call destroying the man-made matrix. These are things that were put into place by a foreign installation, an unnatural mindset as a means to control and amass power. We were born into this world to uphold agreements that empower and feed this foreign installation and it is time to free ourselves from the awareness that is not an innate and natural part of our being.

"We are mindful of the power held by the dark side of the foreign installation in its attempt to sustain its existence by feeding upon the emotions of humanity. Working with male seers we travel through the matrix to see and unravel the lines which consist of all things that do not serve the Earth or her beings. We move among the patterns unwriting thousands of years of conditioning."

As the sun began to set I realized that I had been sitting atop punto intento for the better part of the day. I drank some water, and headed back down the trail to Nayeli's house. It's amazing how the desert comes alive once it cools down as the sun sinks behind the mountains. After so much silence and stillness, a gentle breeze came up and the birds were chirping loudly as they stealthily hunted the insects that emerged from hiding during the hottest time of the day. Quail and their tiny chicks quickly ran for cover upon my approach and lizards darted in every direction as I picked my way through the arroyo once I returned to the base of the hill.

With clarity to my intention and the insight with which to accomplish this task I couldn't wait to talk to Nayeli so I could begin to put my plan into action. When Nayeli first instructed me to recapitulate the dominant paradigm, I didn't understand which direction to go. She told me to do it in a way that requires me to move my assemblage point from its fixated position. Shifting our assemblage point helps us evolve beyond the perceptions that became anchored and practiced over the course of thousands of years.

I felt as though I needed further clarification, but Nayeli never told me what to do or how to do it. She encouraged me to connect with silence, align with Source, and allow for a viable innovation to emerge.

I suggested to her that I accomplish my task by taking advantage of one of the many small caves in the area in order to recapitulate the man-made stories. She laughed heartily saying that caves were for men. Since men didn't have a womb, they had to enter into one in order to touch upon that which a woman already holds in every moment of her waking life. So I countered, requesting that she secure me in a harness high within a tree in the manner that Taisha Abelar, one of the female seers in Carlos Castaneda's group, had undergone her recapitulation. This time Nayeli rolled her eyes and sighed saying that to do it in the same manner that another had undertaken would be to create and maintain a pattern; a foolish move for a seer on a path of total freedom.

Arriving at the house, I walked into the kitchen and without missing a beat, as though I had already shared my revelations and questions, Nayeli said, "Female warriors dance among a myriad of stories within stories. They do this with detachment, ruthlessness, patience, and ease. They meticulously cut through to the core of what it means to live in beauty while aligned with the Earth and the cosmos. Within the fragile yet incredibly strong web of all creation, the harmonic frequency of existence only then, reveals itself. Herein lies total freedom.

"You have to remember, Lorraine, that this arduous yet rewarding work is different for men and women," Nayeli said with utmost seriousness.

"How are they different?" I asked.

"Most men," she explained, "define a point of reference in order to align with Source and strive upwards to achieve that goal. Once they succeed in reaching that point of reference, they create another one and use their will to continually strive upwards. They deepen by going up, traveling along one finite line at a time. Because of their connection to reason, men find comfort in what is tangible and endeavor to know the abstract. They accrue knowledge in a step-by-step fashion, and then attempt to arrange the pieces of the puzzle together to see how it all fits.

"Women, on the other hand," she continued, "are already close to the abstract and deepen into the mastery of intent by opening up to receive numerous lines simultaneously. All a woman has to do to receive knowledge is open to it and Source reaches them directly by exposing multiple lines concurrently. Numerous lines reveal themselves and a woman intuitively sees how each line exists because of another. The womb of a woman is the receptor. Through this direct link with Source energy she realizes that she doesn't have to figure anything out, she just knows. She doesn't become hooked to an idea and then attempt to rationalize it or reason it out."

Hearing it in this way helped to bring further clarity to some of the questions that had arisen while I spent the afternoon sitting atop punto intent. It seemed as though everything was finally coming into focus.

Nayeli continued. "Long ago men recognized that women have a direct link with Spirit and over time they came to resent this beautiful, raw power, wanting it for themselves. Except for males who have already succeeded in aligning with Source, men and even some women continue, after thousands of years, to coerce and even attempt to force women to forget their link with Spirit. The Earth," she said, "has so much to teach and will provide you with knowledge and awareness that surpasses anything you have ever known."

Nayeli is an amazing woman, a double being with a foot in both words. She is an impeccable *nagual* who demanded that I never address her as such. "If you have to refer to me with some limiting definition through a mere word, then just simply call me a seer," she told me.

"But Nayeli, a lot of people see. You have special gifts that clearly indicate your position as a nagual woman," I protested. A nagual, as I understood it from the Castaneda books, was a master of awareness with the ability to assist one in seeing everything in an abstract manner, from the perspective of pure energy or Spirit.

Nayeli eyed me carefully and paused a long time before responding. She sighed deeply and finally said, "If I refer to myself or allow you to refer to me as a nagual woman I will have fixated your attention to a mere label, one that I will never be able to fully live up to based upon the expectations that you hold of what I should come to represent for you. There are men and women popping up everywhere claiming to be naguals. Three-pronged naguals, four-pronged naguals, reincarnated naguals. So much self-importance! Poor Carlitos tried so desperately to free people from the labels and now there is an abundance of people referring to themselves as something they can barely comprehend." I felt Nayeli's passion as she continued.

"The nagual is not a person! It is a flow of energy, the Spirit, an abstract force that cannot be described. It can only be felt. And sometimes, on rare occasions when a warrior is committed to their path with unbending will and discipline, and while continuously practicing the recapitulation, the nagual fills them. It moves through them and all around them, and they become the abstract through their emptiness and resonant vibration.

"I know what I know," she continued, "because I consistently elude the patterns to be free. We cannot be content to understand the unknowable by readings books, skimming the internet, or shifting ourselves into new personas to satisfy ourselves or attempt to fool ourselves into becoming what we simply cannot become. As seers, we can only attempt to become free of the man-made matrix while aligned with intent: with Source energy.

"While I can guide you and support you in your own quest towards freedom, you must come to understand that there is nothing I can tell you that you don't already know. Your freedom comes in making the choices that best suit you. I can bring you to a cave or, I can hoist you into a tree. I can do whatever it is that you would like but I do know that when another's deeds or actions are repeated, they lose power. The expectations one places upon copying another's actions are rarely met and not nearly as fulfilling. The stories of others merely serve as a distraction and create attachments to outcomes that are unlikely to occur. A true warrior is a creator and will put all of their own power behind their commitment to ensure that they are experiencing something fresh and new."

I felt quite humbled and looked down at the ground with a million thoughts racing through my head and nothing to say. Nayeli stood up and put her hand on my shoulder saying, "In order for you to be free, Lorraine, you have to become free of me and your idea of me." I looked into her eyes and saw the abysmal void of infinity, like two black pools of liquid, shining back at me.

The Curandero

Don't blindly follow a path. Forge into the unknown gathering knowledge and awareness along the way. Immerse yourself into the depths of all things so that you may come to know the world through your own passion and not through the vision of another.
- Alejandro

Several months passed since Nayeli and I collected the saguaro fruit, and discussed the practice of recapitulation. I spent the majority of that time recapitulating ceaselessly and could feel the difference it made for me on an energetic level.

I began my practice of recapitulation immediately by hiking up to punto intento and just sitting there, sometimes for hours as I examined the situations in my life to which I had lost energy. Over time, the practice of recapitulation no longer required so much concentration. I would work in the garden, walk on the beach, or dance in the house when some thought would arise. Seizing the moment, I would recapitulate it as it arose.

Early one morning I walked into the kitchen to get some coffee, and Nayeli said, "It's time for you to meet Alejandro so get ready. We're leaving in a half hour." Alejandro was sometimes referred to as the Nagual by a few of the seers in spite of the fact that Nayeli continually attempted to liberate them from referring to him as such.

He was also known as a *curandero*, the Spanish word for healer or shaman. It had been explained to me that his love for the healing energies of plant medicines was strong. He cultivated many herbs and plants for which to aid others into well-being and wholeness. It was said that he could alter one's sense of perception by merely being in his presence.

Trying to mask my anxiety, I told her casually that I wasn't interested in meeting Alejandro or any curandero for that matter. She laughed and told me that I didn't have a choice. He had been waiting patiently, and an omen had presented itself that couldn't be denied.

We drove about five miles from her house and turned onto a driveway that I passed many times. The driveway, nearly a mile long, was lined with giant cottonwood trees on both sides with an irrigation canal running along the right side. We headed towards a modest and beautiful home that was not the typical adobe of the area. It was constructed of smooth, round stones, the type you might find in a river or wash. Brightly colored bougainvillea grew in front of the house, and a beautiful natural dirt path, lined with San Pedro cactus, led to the front door.

I heard that Alejandro was self-sufficient, but it still surprised me to see that there were solar trackers to the right of the house, the kind that follow the direction of the sun. I noticed an old fashioned hand water pump, the type that required you to pump it up and down to create a vacuum suction which then drew water from the well. A small greenhouse was off to one side that, by the looks of it, produced a high yield of vegetables and herbs. Chickens freely wandered around the yard, pecking at insects and weeds.

We parked at the end of the driveway and could see a group of men sitting upon tree stumps and Adirondack chairs under the shade a two huge cottonwood trees. They waved and shouted greetings to Nayeli who waved back. I noticed one man lying in a hammock tied between the trees sitting up awkwardly trying to see us as we approached.

Nayeli brought me directly to an older man that was seated on a big cottonwood stump. Dressed from head to toe in black, he wore black Levi's, a black short-sleeved pocket t-shirt, black baseball cap, and black leather work boots. She bent down to hug him as I stood a few feet away and then she formally introduced us.

"Alejandro, may I present Lorraine, also known as *Nubecita*; Lorraine, this is Alejandro." Reaching forward to shake his hand, I felt as though my hand had become disembodied from my arm.

As our fingers touched he looked into my eyes and like Nayeli's, I found myself looking into the abysmal void of infinity, through two black pools of liquid shining back at me. My ears started to buzz and nothing except the black stillness of that which lay behind his eyes existed. Everything seemed to be moving in slow motion and there were no other people present, only Alejandro and me. It felt as though I began to float while in the deepest state of dream, aware of nothing but emptiness. I could see light but it wasn't bright, it was more like illuminated mist or what it might be like to look through the clouds. An intense feeling of peace spread through my body, and I felt buoyant and unencumbered as I continued to feel myself floating before him.

With my hand still in his, I began to see into the core of

his being, which felt like the center of the universe, and I knew that he was looking into the core of my being. He knew, without having met me before, that I stood in firm resolve of great potential for everyone, for the beauty in everything. He brought me into the center of knowing through a multitude of energetic fibers of awareness that flowed resonantly between us. With great force, he said without words, *keep dancing*, and then he released my hand.

I remained standing there in front of him for what seemed like an eternity until I heard laughter. I felt a snap of consciousness begin to grab hold of me, and I saw Alejandro and the other men slowly begin to emerge from the luminous mist. Alejandro was smiling at me, his black raven eyes glistening like opalescent jewels, and he said softly, "Welcome Nubecita."

As I began to return to my body, still with a foot in both worlds, Nayeli introduced me to the other men. After I met them all, the man in the hammock jumped down, walked over to Nayeli and warmly embraced her. She said, "El Cuervo, meet Nubecita; Nubecita, El Cuervo." As we shook hands, we cocked our heads in the same direction, got lost in each other's eyes for some time and then spoke simultaneously. "Where have you been?" I asked.

"You're real!" he stated.

And the whole group laughed.

After my first encounter with Alejandro, I became much

more relaxed and very quickly grew to admire him deeply. He is a gentle man with a great sense of humor. He weaves stories that push one to zealously explore the boundaries of perception while strengthening their alignment with Source. He communicates with each of us without speaking; what I came to refer to as downloading information to us directly from Spirit, from the universe.

Alejandro has explained to me that although his given name was Alessandro, since moving to Mexico he has adapted it to Alejandro, which is better suited for him as a resident of Mexico. Besides, he says laughing, Alejandro is a much better name for an artist, more poetic. Nayeli fondly calls him *Viejo* which means old man, but she says it with joy and deep affection, and he receives it in the same manner. They've known each other for many years, and though they live in separate homes they have the comfort of a long-time married couple.

Alejandro is a quiet yet exuberant man, a humble man, and likes nothing more than to sit under the shade of the cottonwood trees, listening to the birds and closely watching whatever reveals itself. He has an uncanny ability to become invisible. One will walk over towards the cottonwood trees to lie in the hammock or sit in the shade and won't even see Alejandro until they are right next to him. He blends into his surroundings and always laughs heartily when his unseen presence causes someone to jump in startled surprise when he makes himself visible.

It's not that he actually becomes invisible in spite of the fact that it most certainly appears that way. He is so impeccable with his energy, so totally still within and without his entire being that his presence is often imperceptible.

An Italian American fluent in Spanish, English, and Italian, Alejandro is proud of the fact that he is an expatriate artist, having given up his ties to the US many years ago and settling into his Mexico home. He told me that he fell in love with Mexico the first time he visited, almost 40 years prior to me meeting him. Ten years later, after he had saved enough money from selling his artwork, he sold almost all of his belongings and bought the property on which he had constructed his home and has been living there ever since. His house, and Nayeli's too for that matter, are essentially galleries of the beautiful abstract and unique art that he constantly works on when he isn't sitting outside listening to the birds or creating yard art with the many stones and natural elements that are so readily available throughout the area. With dark skin and hair and eyes almost black, he looks Hispanic and easily passes as a local.

One afternoon, several weeks after our introduction, I brought lunch to him as he sat alone quietly under the trees. He smiled as I approached and said, "You must have read my mind, I just thought about how nice it would be to have something to eat."

I smiled and sat down on the chair next to him. He squeezed some lime and poured some hot sauce on his meal. Using a warm corn tortilla, he scooped up some of the sardines, fresh tomatoes, and onions on his plate. He ate everything with lime and hot sauce, even popcorn. "The morning that I met you Nayeli told me that an omen presented itself to you indicating that it was time to meet me. What was the omen?" I asked.

He considered this for a few moments before answering.

"Didn't Nayeli tell you?" he asked.

"No," I said, "she didn't say a word."

"Hmmm, just like her to leave you hanging," he laughed then explained. "I told Nayeli about a dream that I had. In this dream, a girl around your age was traveling through the desert. She was dancing between the worlds, on the razor's edge of reality as she knows it and the mystery that she was exploring. Her awareness was increasing and she kept asking a lot of questions, to no one in particular. Next thing I know, a gigantic dust devil rose up from the desert taking the girl with it. The dust devil turned into a big spiraling cloud and from it emerged a serpent with the girl on its back. They rode along the surface of the earth and then up to the stars and back to the earth again."

I hung on Alejandro's every word recalling my own dream about a spiraling cloud and a serpent. "What happened next?" I asked.

"Damnedest thing. I anticipated what was going to happen next and then I woke up," he said simply and returned to his meal.

"You're messing with me, aren't you?" I asked, very frustrated because I thought he would be providing me with more insights about my dream. I felt as though he had more to tell me and was holding back.

He laughed heartily and said, "No, I'm not messing with you. It was an odd dream, unlike any I have ever had. When I relayed this dream to Nayeli she told me that it was time for me to meet you because you had a similar dream."

"What does this dream mean?" I asked.

After he took another mouthful and slowly savored it he

said, "In all honesty, I don't know. What I do know is now that you've met me, you know there is nothing I can tell you."

I told him that Nayeli said something similar to me but I didn't understand what she meant. "What do you mean there is nothing you can tell me? I venture to guess that with all of your life's experience and wisdom there are millions of things you can tell me. How will I learn to deepen on my path if you don't tell me things?" I asked, almost in a state of panic thinking he didn't believe in my potential to grow beyond what I already diligently practiced.

He laughed again and said, "Well, Nubecita, that's entirely up to you."

My ears began to buzz, which over time became common when I found myself in his presence. I felt a familiar feeling of weightlessness. Sound lost its distinction, there were no identifiable songs of birds, cicadas or the light breeze flowing through the leaves of the trees. All sounds became one, like a wind tunnel moving through me and around me at the same time. I turned my head slowly to look at Alejandro and was surprised but not startled to see him, not as a man, but as an elongated orb with a golden glow all around him. From the orb that he had become were millions of gossamer threads flowing out in all directions. I turned my focus from him to look down at myself and saw the same luminous fibers emanating from me. It made me dizzy for a moment, and without words I heard him say, "Don't analyze or try to rationalize it. Just surrender."

As I looked out across the yard, I saw similar fibers coming from and connecting to all things. The one sound of all sounds continued to move through me and around me. I watched with wonder as my luminous fibers were merging with Alejandro's luminous fibers and then merging with the fibers of all other things around us. I found myself getting up from my chair, not standing, more like just rising while being supported by all of the lines of energy that I connected with. The next thing I knew I stood at the base of one of the giant cottonwood trees, watching it pulsate in the same glowing energy and I put my hands, which were more like emanations of energy, upon her trunk. Within seconds I sat on her lowest branch amazed at the oneness I felt with all things.

A very subtle pulsating sensation was moving through my body and seemed to be coming from the tree. I heard what I thought was Alejandro saying, "Ride the lines of awareness," and then I felt a pulsation coming from the Earth, into the tree and into me. As I sat on the branch, I began to feel what can only be described as a steady heartbeat moving through both of us as well as the Earth, the trees, the bugs, the birds, the blades of grass, the stones and reaching deep into the sky.

I heard a distant voice. "There is nothing anyone can tell you. If you align with Source, you will be in the moment without the distractions of the past or the future, then you begin to truly see and perceive things in a most incredible and new way. It is at this moment that you are completely aligned with Source and the silent knowledge that allows you to know that you already know."

The lines I saw slowly began to fade, and I heard birds chirping above me. As I returned from a heightened state of awareness, I noticed that Alejandro was standing below me looking up at me smiling and said, "Hang on with both hands, Nubecita. I don't want you to startle yourself and fall." I got my bearings and realized with astonishment that I sat on a branch in the tree. "How did I get up here?" I inquired quietly, a little disconcerted about my situation.

"I think you fell in love with the tree," he laughed. "Suddenly you were moving towards the tree, placed your hands on her trunk and were buoyed up onto her branches."

I jumped about six feet down on wobbly legs and said, "What just happened to me?"

"When seers have the energy and power to align with Source," he explained, "there we stand looking into and feeling into the unknown, the abyss, the void. Floating in complete surrender. And then something magical begins to occur. The veil lifts, so to speak, and the conditioning that prevents one from seeing, feeling, sensing, knowing, intuiting things as they really are is gone."

"This is a power deal, Nubecita, to unite in gratitude with the awareness of the Earth. To sit upon her in silence and connect with the pulse of the Earth, for it is inner silence that induces the displacement of the assemblage point, ours and hers. And through this mutual power deal, the Earth and you shall pulse with those combined energies. In so doing you will have connected with silent knowledge, will be more attuned to yourself, and will know that there is nothing anyone can teach you that you don't already have full access to."

Inorganic Beings and Allies

> Sometimes an inorganic being appears; alone or in groups and they murmur. Suddenly you realize that they are trying to figure out how to get some of your energy. You want to run, but you really can't because they'll chase you. They love the chase! You must exercise self-control, detachment and courage to hold your ground. When you do, they will go away, and your personal power will increase.
> - Alejandro

One morning as I walked out of Nayeli's house I saw El Cuervo walking purposefully across the backyard carrying a toolbox. He is an amazing dreamer, and ever since our introduction to each other at Alejandro's house we have spent a lot of time together. He and I began travelling often throughout the southwestern United States and Sonora, Mexico, leisurely driving on the back roads, as is our preference to taking the interstate. It was both surprising and plausible to learn that we each had a home in Phoenix. There are no accidents in the warrior's world.

I followed him to his pick-up and stood near the driver's side as he popped the hood.

"*Que onda, Nubecita?*" he said asking me how it was going. I always smiled when he called me that. Nubecita means little cloud, a term of endearment that Nayeli gave to me as a result of the dream I had of the cloud serpent. The nickname given to El Cuervo by Alejandro means the raven, and the seers call us by these names.

We quickly became nearly inseparable, and as a result we were the brunt of a lot of jokes among the warriors. "El Cuervo has his head in the clouds" was a favorite among them. When we approached them together, someone would always say it, and the guffaws and belly laughs that followed still bring a slight blush to my cheeks. I am far from bashful, but the innuendos never cease to embarrass me. It was evident that their pleasure was derived from my discomfort.

"I've packed a cooler with some snacks and beverages in the hopes that I could talk you into a trip to the mountains," I said while hoping he would be in agreement to this little trip that I wanted to take for some time.

"Which mountains?" El Cuervo asked knowing full well which mountains I wanted to explore.

"*The* mountains. You know, the *mountains*. The mountains that are said to contain all of the enchantment and magic," I said playfully.

"Well your timing couldn't be better," he said, "I have nothing planned for the entire day and would love to accompany you. Ready when you are!"

There are moments when the assemblage point is so fluid that a shift into dream comes without warning. One moment you are lucid and functioning as one would expect in the tonal, the state of everyday awareness, the world of reason and descriptions, when suddenly everything shifts and the nagual takes over.

El Cuervo and I were heading north from Nayeli's house

in Southern Sonora when such a shift occurred. It engulfed me swiftly and though I could barely talk, I uttered to El Cuervo that everything was out of focus. The road wavered and it took me great effort to steer the pick-up. He told me to pull to the side of the road and stop. I turned off the ignition and stepped out of the pick-up on wobbly legs. Everything felt thick, like walking through water without getting wet.

"El Cuervo, what's happening to me?" I asked in a panic.

"You have entered into an extraordinary state of heightened awareness. This is not surprising at all considering our close proximity to the Bacatete Mountains. It must be the *Surem* probing you. We'll be in the foothills very soon; they are aware of your approach," he said.

I felt extremely disconcerted and had never so fully entered dream while driving before. Even the quality of the desert was somewhat different from how I had always known it to be. Everything looked softer, the plants were greener, the cactus and trees seemed taller, and it was so still; not a sound could be heard.

It was impossible for me to ground, and El Cuervo abruptly jumped in the driver's seat, started the vehicle and shouted, "What're you waiting for, jump in!"

He was exhibiting a sense of exhilaration and excitement that seemed so foreign to his usual composed and serene manner. He hit the accelerator so fast that the tires squealed and a spray of gravel shot up behind us as we pulled back onto the highway. He started singing loudly and would slap my thigh from time to time in rhythm with his tune. Driving faster than was typical for him I asked pointedly, "El Cuervo, what is going on, why are you in such a hurry?"

I nearly jumped out of my skin when he abruptly shouted, "There is something incredible waiting and we have no time to waste," reminding me momentarily of Nayeli.

And then he laughed with so much abandon and joy that I found myself giggling with him in spite of the surrealism of everything that was happening. "If we don't take immediate action we might miss it completely," he said.

I started to ask him what the Surem are, and he held up his hand and said, "Silencio! We have to pay attention to everything." It was out of character for him to be so abrupt, but I took it to be part of his excitement and couldn't help but wonder what we were getting into in these so-called magical and enchanting mountains.

Once we were at the edge of the town he turned down a dirt road and headed towards the mountains. Besides the dry, sandy washes and desert there were only rocks, cactus, mesquite and palo verde trees on gently sloping hills.

After driving for about ten minutes, El Cuervo stopped the pick-up, got out and started walking as though he was just taking an afternoon stroll. Still in a state of heightened awareness, and not sure what to do, I got out and started to walk in a different direction from him. I looked at the ground, as was my habit to look for beautiful stones; on occasion I would find arrowheads, pottery shards or crystals.

We were in the middle of nowhere, a vast desert with little vegetation. It was hot and still as I gazed up at the rugged mountain range to my right. The ground was littered with rocks, small stones and pebbles and it occurred to me that all sound had ceased. Not a bird or a breeze. Not even a cicada which is so unusual in the heat of the desert. Several small dust devils were rising up from the desert floor and climbing towards the sky like miniature tornadoes in reverse. I watched as one in the distance grew large and suddenly gathered speed and seemed to be heading in our direction.

El Cuervo walked quietly with his hands behind his back, and I had not spoken since he silenced me. I wanted to get his attention so he could see the approaching dust devil, but I couldn't speak. It was very close to bringing a dust storm into our direction when it abruptly rose higher with great force and dissipated. I suddenly became very aware of people whispering all around me. My eyes wide, I quickly searched in every direction trying to discern where the voices were coming from. I realized they were all around me even though no one else was in sight besides El Cuervo.

"El Cuervo!" I shouted.

He calmly said, "Just keep walking."

I shouted in panic, "but there are voices all around us and they're talking about us. Can't you hear them? We'd better go! We'd better get back to the pick-up, they're going to get us!"

He ordered me to stop feeding my fear, to pay attention and to relax. My panic swelled. It terrified me to not know what was around us while the chatter increased and grew louder. With a look of panic on my face and about to break into a run, El Cuervo said very firmly: "Calm down! I have never known you to exhibit so much fear. They are becoming energized from your emotions. Allow them to satisfy their curiosity about you. Do what you do best and dance with them."

I stood still and started to breath steadily, which always worked to calm me, but this time was different. I couldn't bear the noise, the constant unintelligible muffled babble that was pressing on me from all directions including the ground and the sky. Despite El Cuervo's warnings, I walked quickly to the pick-up, opened the passenger door and got in. I heard him laughing with glee as he started to walk slowly over to my side of the truck.

What the heck is going on? I asked myself. I keep expecting people to begin emerging from the desert, but I know that isn't going to happen. I have never in my life experienced anything like this. What is it, I wondered?

As if reading my mind El Cuervo said, "These are the Surem, and they apparently have quite an interest in you. You should consider yourself fortunate that they are dancing around you so boldly. They are timid beings who typically hide unless they want to frighten someone away."

"Well, they have certainly succeeded in frightening me, even if that isn't their intention," I replied. The desert was beginning to quiet down, and it felt as though they were losing interest in our presence. I too was beginning to relax and asked El Cuervo who or what the Surem are.

"The Surem," he began with a bright sparkle in his eyes, "are the Spirits of the Bacatete Mountains. Though there are several myths and folklore surrounding them, we know them as beings that have lived in another time, beings who have harmonized their intent so exquisitely that they were able to assemble a new band of awareness in which to live. Through their combined alignment with Source, they are able to move from band to band at will and with ease. You have surely piqued their curiosity, and they saw you approaching from miles away."

"Did you hear them? It was like they were all talking at once, did you understand what they were saying?" I asked. He threw his head back and laughed, his long black hair flying behind him in the wind that had just kicked up from the North. He went on to tell me that they recognize a very specific amber glow that emanates from warriors. Since they themselves have harmonized their intent, they can perceive the glow from within their own band. As curious creatures they will sometimes energetically amass to check it out. "That's why they were chattering so much, they like to come to this band to visit but they don't unless they have good reason."

"Are they inorganic beings?" I asked.

"Yes, they are inorganic beings but more than that, the Surem are allies," he said.

I had never been completely clear on the difference between inorganic beings and allies but I asked him anyway, hoping he wouldn't consider me to be completely dense on the subject.

"Good question," he said making me feel more at ease. "Inorganic beings don't have physical form but they are fields of energy that hold awareness. They are present on the Earth and exist beyond time and space. They may have had form at some point and may incarnate into form if they so desire. They travel through the great sea of awareness accessing the past, present, and future to gather knowledge and increase awareness."

"When we die will we become inorganic beings?" I asked.

Laughing El Cuervo replied, "Yes, I suppose we will."

"So what is an ally then? Isn't an ally an inorganic being too?" I asked wondering if this would ever make sense to me.

"OK," he said. "An ally is an inorganic being but kind of like, um, with an agenda. They appear to warriors to bring them knowledge or to help them to enter into heightened states of awareness. An ally often shows up when a warrior needs assistance in seeing, or in some cases to stop their world. There are lots of energetic entities in the universe. Some are referred to as ghosts, angels, Spirit beings, helpers; a whole host of definitions and meanings.

"What an ally does is help you to gain and strengthen your awareness so you can enter into other dimensions of power besides this one. An ally can help you to recognize and understand awareness in realities that exist beyond the physical and can guide you from first attention, a world of descriptions, and into second attention, a place of pure perception. They are even known to work cooperatively with people and make power deals with them. They are able to approach a warrior that they have identified as such due to the amount of luminous fibers that they emit. That's how they recognized you; by the amount of energy that you emanate.

"The Surem are kind of like highly evolved allies," he continued. "It is said that they once embodied form, just like you and I do, and as dedicated warriors, they became so impeccable with their energy that they concurrently left the Earth and reassembled energetically and without form into a new band of awareness of their own creation. When our awareness is aligned with other energetic forces of the universe we are capable of becoming a force of power through the fibrous lines of energy that lie within reach of our own emanations. And then, we have the ability to create through intention alone."

"What exactly is a band of awareness?" I asked.

"Think of the Earth as a band of awareness. It is a node of awareness within the universe that is capable of hosting all kinds of organic beings. It is made up of luminous fibers and energetic emanations to which other organic and even inorganic awareness may attach. The Surem are capable of creating a reality through the energetic emanations of their own awareness, a world of luminous fibers of their own design."

I tried hard to comprehend what he was telling me, but it was difficult since so much had happened in such a short period of time. I had become much more relaxed and turned to face forward in the passenger seat while El Cuervo stood under the sparse shade of a palo verde tree on the passenger side of the truck. Suddenly, without warning, another gust of wind blew fiercely from the north causing me to shiver in spite of the increasing temperature as the day grew hotter.

"Look El Cuervo," I nearly yelled, "there is a man coming towards us with a burro!" A tremor of fear took hold of me once again as I saw a tall, lean man walking beside a burro in our direction from the north. He was wearing a sombrero and was dressed in all white clothing. I squinted to see them more clearly, but they were far off in the distance and remained blurry.

El Cuervo ran off into the desert, and I turned to see where he was going, horrified that he might be abandoning me due to his own fear. He suddenly bent down, picked something up and came running back to the pick-up. I looked towards the man and the burro again and though they seemed to be coming closer they were no nearer than they were when I first saw them.

"Quickly," El Cuervo practically shouted, "you must make a bundle to put this tiny stone in." He handed me the tiny stone and told me to sew it up. I swiftly pulled out my travel pouch containing a sewing kit holding little squares of fabric, a needle, and thread. I rapidly sewed the stone into a piece of blue fabric while constantly looking up to watch the man and the burro. They were still walking but contrary to what it seemed, they were not getting any closer to us.

It was a miracle that I finished sewing the bundle without piercing myself with the needle. El Cuervo said, "Good, now attach a cord to the bundle in the fashion of a neck thong so you can wear it." I did as he asked and handed it to him. He briefly inspected it and then quickly put it around my neck.

"What is this for?" I asked.

He said, "The man and the burro who are still approaching us without getting closer are luminous beings and are offering a great gift to us. He wants to travel in this band again in exchange for awareness. Consider it a power deal."

"A power deal for what?" I asked.

"To travel!" he exclaimed. "He wants to travel within this Earthly realm and as such will provide us with access to unlimited energy so that we may explore and deepen into other dimensions of awareness that lie beyond this Earth! What a gift! We'll call him 'the Traveler.'"

"What do you mean, he wants to travel? He's an inorganic being, an ally. Can't he just move through the Earth energetically?" I asked, more confused than ever.

"Allies desire to increase their awareness through human awareness. They are more than willing to provide energy in exchange for human awareness. They can move over the Earth energetically, but unless they are connected with a warrior, they are unable to access the awareness that they seek."

I had more questions than answers and told El Cuervo that fear was taking its toll and I wanted to leave. At that moment we lost sight of the man and the burro as they briefly descended into a wash. On the next rise they appeared, once again, without being any closer to us.

El Cuervo walked to his side of the truck and got in. He started the pick-up as I returned the contents to my travel pouch, and made a U-turn heading back down the dirt road in the direction from which we came. We were quiet, and I sat there trying to make sense of all that had happened when suddenly, El Cuervo laughed and said, "I have never, ever seen you so frightened of anything before. It was different and refreshing to witness you in such a vulnerable mood."

I didn't know for sure if he was mocking me so I told him that I had been terrified. He said that when and if you ever have the good fortune to be in the midst of the pure and curious beings that are the Surem, the only thing you should do is dance with them. I told him I'd keep that in mind.

That evening I told Nayeli about the events in the desert with the Surem and the Traveler and was hoping that she would be able to provide me with more clarity. She was so excited to learn of this and said that it was the perfect omen.

"Perfect omen for what?" I asked wondering what she had in store for me this time. Nayeli was strongly connected to omens and whenever one presented itself, it usually meant that something momentous was about to occur.

"A traveling ally, that is brilliant!" she exclaimed. "It doesn't surprise me that the Traveler has made a deal with you and El Cuervo. The way that you two love to drive all over the place exploring everything was most likely the impetus for this deal to occur. This ally has probably been following the two of you for quite some time, waiting for just the right moment to approach you. It is very fortuitous that you went to the mountains when you did. Your timing was impeccable."

"What does that mean, why was the timing impeccable?"

"Do you remember the first time you met Alejandro?" she asked. I nodded. "Remember how you wound up sitting in the tree?" I nodded again. "Well, as I recall you told me that he spoke to you about uniting with the awareness of the Earth and to ride the lines of awareness. The ally is providing you with the energy necessary to stalk awareness so you can recapitulate the repetitive patterns of humanity. It knows that your task will take you to many places and it wants to go with you to learn more about the Earth. It wants to align with your awareness in order to gain more energy. And in return, it is providing you with the energy and awareness you require to accomplish your task," she said.

I shook my head. "Wow, Nayeli, that sounds really intense and maybe a bit bigger than I bargained for."

"Don't be silly," she said. "You have been diligent in your practice and the omen is letting you know that it is time for you to amass the energy necessary so that you may completely align with intent. Accept this gift, give gratitude for it, and allow yourself the opportunity that you are being given to dance along all the lines of awareness. You are going to be uniting with the web of creation."

Moving Beyond Illusion

When you look deeply into the wilderness, so deep that
you feel your own wild and primal self, you begin to
understand the immensity of material illusion.
- El Cuervo

The sun was just coming up as I awoke, and I found myself walking to Alejandro's house while contemplating the journey that I wanted to take to the southwestern states of Arizona and Utah. After my conversation with Nayeli about the gift of energy that the Traveler was offering us, I anxiously anticipated the next part of my journey.

I looked forward to uniting with the awareness of the earth ever since Alejandro first mentioned it to me that day under the cottonwood trees. Now, after having recapitulated so much of the personal stuff in my life, I felt truly ready to embark upon my task.

As I walked down Alejandro's driveway, it occurred to me how early it was and I wondered if anyone was awake. I heard some sounds coming from the pickup truck, parked by the house, and saw the hood was up. Sure enough, El Cuervo was tinkering with something under the hood. To ensure that I didn't startle him I said good morning as I approached the truck and walked over to where he was working.

"You look like the cat that swallowed the canary," he said

while adjusting something in the engine with a pair of pliers. "What's up?"

"Are you ready for a road trip?" I asked knowing that he would be more than happy to venture out. He is a wanderer, always ready to explore the new and the unknown.

"When do we leave, Nubecita?" he asked with a twinkle in his eyes as he lowered the hood of the pick-up.

That evening, Nayeli, Alejandro, and a couple of the other seers helped El Cuervo and me celebrate our departure to the United States. The two of us would be leaving at dawn. We had a wonderful dinner that we all created together. I rarely ate meat, but Nayeli made a wonderful pot of *carnitas*, pulled pork in red chili sauce that she slow-cooked all afternoon. She purchased her meat from a local farmer and I knew I couldn't resist tasting it as soon as the aroma hit me. A salad made of fresh tomatoes, cucumbers and basil from Nayeli's garden dressed with olive oil and lime was made by someone else, as were the warm, homemade corn tortillas. My contribution was flan; I learned how to make this simple and decadent dessert from Nayeli. El Cuervo knew Nayeli's and my weakness for dark chocolate with strawberries, and they were a great compliment to the flan.

The next morning, as El Cuervo and I put our few belongings in the back of the pick-up, Nayeli said, "Call me when you can. In fact, Nubecita, have you considered keeping a journal or even a blog of your travels? I think you should write everything down, and then after you've had a chance to review and appraise it all, you can recapitulate it. If you create a blog, I will be able to read your entries while you are on the traveling throughout your journey."

I have never kept a written record of anything, no journals or diaries, it wasn't my thing, but I told her that I'd take her advice into consideration.

El Cuervo hugged Nayeli, and then she and I embraced. She whispered in my ear, "Connect with the Earth; she will boost you beyond your wildest dreams. The alignment of her emanations with yours will deliver you into the amazing net of oneness, with humility, gratitude, and utter simplicity. This net, this web of creation, is where all dreams and visions are born, and from where we have the freedom to assemble our new reality in order to dance awake our own dream."

Wiping warm tears that filled my eyes after hearing her powerful statement, I climbed into the pick-up with El Cuervo, and we drove off waving to Nayeli as we pulled from the driveway and onto the asphalt.

Sensing my pensive mood, El Cuervo drove for quite some time in silence. I felt so happy and relieved that he agreed to accompany me on my warrior's task. When I told him about it, he was excited and remarked that Alejandro had recently advised him to engage in a similar undertaking. While my task was to stalk awareness while recapitulating the patterns and the man-made stories, El Cuervo was to reveal the common link that lies at the root of all paradigms. It was, as always, a complimentary match, and I couldn't help but wonder if Nayeli and Alejandro intended these tasks for each of us to work through together.

I thought about Nayeli's response to what happened to me

with Alejandro when I wound up sitting on the lower branch of the cottonwood tree. "You must honor the Earth at all times. She is our ultimate source and our greatest ally. It's important that you deepen your connection with her because it is she who will nurture you, protect you, and energize you. You must connect with the pulse of the Earth, her very heartbeat itself."

She had gone on to explain that the stillness and peace of the desert, including its allies, teaches us how to enter into the silence within. She also said that recapitulating the personal is so effective in the desert because there are few distractions.

I recalled Nayeli saying, "Since you have spent so much time recapitulating the personal, you are empty enough to begin recognizing the patterns of the world through the pulse of the Earth and all its life. As you travel away from the Sonoran desert, the noises and constant movement will show you how.

"You must learn to exercise and hone your awareness in ways that are different from the desert, because other environments are powerful and can consume you if you do not pay attention. It is within those environments outside of the desert that you will learn to stalk quietly by allowing the power of the desert that lives within you to emerge. Your silence will allow you to remain fluid amidst the commotion that may unfold."

Before I knew it, we were getting our passports ready and approaching the border in Nogales. El Cuervo told me that once we got through, we'd head towards Tucson to gas up and get something to eat. We would each be staying at our respective residences in Phoenix for the night to regroup, repack, and sleep before we ventured out again the next day.

Once we passed through the border I asked El Cuervo to

explain to me what he thought about the tasks that we had each been assigned.

He remained silent for so long I began to wonder if he was going to answer me. Finally, he said, "A warrior's drive towards freedom is grounded in their ability to perceive in new ways. When we allow our assemblage points to become fluid and live fully in the moment, we begin to recognize the futility of attempting to maintain the patterns of humanity."

My head started to spin as I envisioned the magnitude of this task with clarity. I had been focused on recapitulating the man-made stories more as moving into a state of total detachment from them. Now finally, the impact of Nayeli's statement hit me full force. "This is your task," she had said, "to stalk awareness while ceaselessly recapitulating the patterns of humanity. This will allow you to align with the emanations of the Earth. You will come to know her stories and dance along those lines for as far back as they will take you. She will energize you so that you will be able to recapitulate the stories of the Earth."

Yes, the magnitude of this monumental task began to make sense. The way I understood it was that once we succeed in reclaiming the energy that we had expended in aligning with the social order, we will have the power necessary to recapitulate the stories that perpetuate the illusions that hold the Earth's inhabitants as prisoners.

"But how can I even begin to recapitulate the repetitive patterns of man-made stories? And why would I want to?" I exclaimed with frustration. "I've spent so much time recapitulating my own life so that my assemblage point may become fluid."

El Cuervo laughed and said, "*Cálmate*, Nubecita, don't get yourself all worked up."

I did calm down, as he had stated, by connecting with my breath and multiple lines started to emerge before my eyes. The stories, the patterns of the world revealed themselves right before me. I began to witness what looked like some kind of spectator sport. People, who were standing inside an enclosed, fenced-in area, watched others who were running as fast as they could, as though trying to break free of something. They were running at full speed towards a finish line with the ferocious gleam of freedom in their eyes. The spectators who were inside the fenced-in area cheered them on, rejoicing at their victory. Yet the people inside the fenced area chose to remain behind the fence.

I took a closer look at the people who stood within the fence and saw through their temporary cheerfulness, a deeply ingrained sadness, even despair. I wanted to yell to them, "run, run," but I knew in my heart that they wouldn't. Even though they were happy to watch those who would choose to break free of the chains of bondage, their assemblage points were so fixated that they did not have the courage or energy to attempt to liberate themselves. So strong was the safety net of stories that they had assembled as their reality. It seemed as though their fear was grounded in their unprecedented need to conform to something they didn't even know or understand, keeping them imprisoned within a state of compliance and reason.

I became aware of the fact that I still sat in the front seat of the pick-up and explained to El Cuervo what I had just aligned with.

"Those who were running away were doing so because

consensus is of no importance to a warrior," El Cuervo replied. "When a warrior steps outside of the place of reason, they become free from attachment and secure in the totality of their autonomous authenticity. Aligned with Source, they are moved strictly by Spirit. Sometimes, exercising free will can include going against the flow, and a warrior learns to discern."

"Sometimes I get so overwhelmed," I admitted to El Cuervo. "It's kind of like, what is the point to all of this? Ignorance is bliss, and I sometimes wish I could be just like everyone else. Maybe I could become a little sheep within the giant flock of acquiescent people who just hide behind the veil of ignorance while going through the motions. It's kind of like the more access I have to awareness, the more things just become increasingly painful. When you consider that we are all one, that we are all united in Spirit, that we come from the one universal source energy, it becomes difficult to witness so much violence and greed occurring in the world. Humanity is out of control and it makes me so sad."

Mostly an upbeat person, I have always been able to look at the bright side of things and recognize that our reality is of our own creation. I worked diligently to distance myself from the horrible realities that were constantly being created and co-created by others in the world, and I understood that these are the very stories that I had to recapitulate. Having put myself into a melancholy mood, I said to El Cuervo that I had grown so tired of the terrible things that humans do to each other, to the Earth, to the animals.

He told me that I was experiencing the deepest levels of compassion, the ones that pulled so hard at your heart that it sometimes became difficult to breathe.

"The Earth," he explained, "is the planet on which we, as pure consciousness, decided to take form. We wanted to explore life in human form, and we chose this beautiful Earth on which to do it. We must pay homage to the Earth for her stately beauty, her selfless giving, and her constant acts of creation. She energizes us, soothes and heals us, and assists us in raising our levels of awareness and consciousness. In order to attain states of heightened awareness and higher levels of consciousness, we must be sure to embrace our opportunity to build a strong foundation on stable ground. Like trees, the more deeply rooted we become in the Earth, the more support we have for expansion.

"Being on the Earth provides us with a holistic and instinctive tendency to enter into a state of natural balance. It is through our connection with the Earth that we are able to heighten our level of consciousness. Our attention increases and we are able to perceive in a new and pure manner."

"What you're saying," I asked tentatively, "is that when we connect deeply and in gratitude to the Earth, the cosmic Source energy of all creation awakens within us, allowing us to cross the bridge that exists between the Earth and the Spirit?"

"Yes," he said. "Our connection with the Earth allows us to align with our original universal energy source bringing us into a state of universal oneness. It is here that we are able to embody the grandeur, wholeness, and unity from which we emerged. When we align with the Earth, an energy balancing takes place which realigns us and returns us to our true nature. We then become free of the patterns of humanity with the innate ability to truly live as the self-empowered and creative beings that we are."

I asked El Cuervo to pull into the upcoming rest area. I needed to get out of the confines of the pick-up and walk with my feet on the Earth so I could incorporate this information into my body. We went over to the partial shade of a mesquite tree at the edge of the parking lot. After a few minutes of walking around stretching my arms and legs, I said, "So, if everything that happens to us happens to the Earth and vice versa, humanity could wind up destroying the whole creation."

El Cuervo nodded silently.

"Humanity is out of control," I repeated, "consumed by greed and in turn consuming everything and everyone without the slightest bit of awareness about the web of life. The Earth has become part of this consumption. If we continue to deplete her resources, she may indeed become a barren wasteland as her fresh waters dry up and her oceans die and her forests are demolished. This would ultimately prevent human life from hydrating and breathing.

"Then what we wind up with is dead planet that can no longer sustain life. We might as well live on Mars or the moon in that case. If the Earth dies it may continue to exist in spite of its death but our source of energy would die and the ability to live upon her in a state of symbiosis would die along with it."

El Cuervo looked at me with a sadness in his eyes and said, "Yes, Nubecita. If the Earth, our source, ceases to exist, then the energy that sustains life on this planet ceases to exist because there is nothing left to power it up. While we may become Spirits, inorganic beings, or pure consciousness when our human form dies, if the Earth dies, the power source that has the ability to host human awareness upon it dies as well. The Earth," he continued, "needs to be perceived and honored as it was intended to be; as part of the journey and not the destination.

"What is important for a warrior is to ensure that we are not losing our energy to the discord and imbalance. If we do, the position of our assemblage point may become fixated, and as a result we may find ourselves immersed in the constant bombardment of thoughts that go through our minds. We cannot allow the madness of the monkey mind to have power over us, or we may wind up operating from a point of reason rather than operating from a place of power with fluidity.

He gently went on, "I think that is why we were given the tasks we were given. As we continue to increase our awareness, we must simultaneously let go of everything and connect, once again, to the flow of power. Our states of heightened awareness will remind us that everything in the physical world, the world of the tonal, is an illusion that we can move beyond. It is through the stories of the Earth that we come to understand the suffering of the world that is brought about by the forces of darkness. We will see the common link to all the stories, and then we will recapitulate every last one of them. We will confront the patterns and man-made stories head on, and then we will change the agreements that we have unwittingly made in order to uphold those patterns."

I had calmed down considerably and everything that El Cuervo said made perfect sense. "So you're basically saying that the energy we reclaim as a result of recapitulating those stories will free us so that we can create and exist in freedom."

"Exactly. The battle that we must each undertake is the fight within ourselves, to continually work at eliminating the feelings that arise within each of us that make us feel that we are separate from the Source. When we are able to accomplish the task of aligning with Source energy, we find that we are able to live in a state of profound harmony with everything. This allows us to exist effortlessly in the flow of the cosmos as it moves continuously around us at all times while recognizing that most stories of man are an illusion."

"Our combined task then," I offered, "is to release what we know in order to face the unknown, to dance seamlessly between the tonal and the nagual. To find peace while we are constantly engaged in battle, and to find the resolve that allows us to become effortlessly fluid. The key," I concluded, "is in becoming impeccable with our energy."

The Voice of Seeing

Life is constantly unfolding all around us. The deeper into it that we look, the more aware we become. When we become aware of what is sitting right in front of us, we are able to comprehend what is swimming in the sea of awareness.
- Alejandro

It was the morning of our departure from Phoenix, and El Cuervo helped me put my tent and belongings in his pick-up. We began our drive towards the Four Corners area. We decided to add New Mexico to our travels and drive into Chaco Canyon on the eastern edge of the Navajo Indian reservation where we would relax and camp for the evening.

Chaco Canyon is one of the largest and most complex concentrations of ruins in the Southwest, and we had been to this particular site several times before. You could feel the ancestral energy of the place teeming from the cliffs. It was, for the most part, an intense energy that had the propensity to keep you fully aware and on guard at all times.

Besides the pictographs and petroglyphs that are found throughout the ruins, there are doorways that I refer to as portals, built in the shape of T's that connect multiple dwellings to each other. It is believed that the T-shape represents a doorway to the Spirit world, and that the construction of them was brought to this region from the ancient Mayans since the T-shaped doorways are found in many of their ruins and temples. The T-shape is also used to indicate ceremonial spaces and altars.

The Anasazi or Ancestral Pueblo people built these along with many other cliff dwellings scattered throughout the Southwest region of the United States. These people occupied southwestern areas from as far back as 7,000 B.C.

We drove to an area of the ruins that had multiple structures connected by these T-shaped doorways and entered them so we could sit in the shade. It felt good to put our backpacks down after bending to get through three successive T-doorways. I spread a small blanket and unpacked a bag of pita chips and the hummus and tabouli that I had prepared the night before.

There were no other people around and the place was intensely quiet. After we ate, we sat across from each other with our backs against the cool adobe walls talking about our own ideas about the people who had occupied these ruins. Suddenly, without warning, a woman screamed at the top of her lungs, "DREAM!"

I jumped up from my place and was practically sitting on top of El Cuervo as a young Indian woman walked through the low T-doorway fully upright and stopped to stand directly in front of us. She just stood there looking at us for what seemed to be a very long and uncomfortable time. Then she put her hand over her heart, closed her eyes briefly and sat down across from us in the center of the ruin we were in.

She was barely five feet tall, judging from the approximate height of the doorway, and she was very dark skinned with course black hair cut straight across her shoulders. She didn't have any shoes on and wore a simple cotton dress with an amulet made of leather hanging around her neck. It obviously held some small objects because it was lumpy and we could see the contours of items through the well-worn pouch.

She stared at us for a very long time, her jet-black eyes glistening like a raven's. We were looking at her too, and I offered her my water bottle. She shook her head no and smiled.

The walls of the small room we were sitting in began to dissolve and a surreal, dream-like quality encompassed us. The women's hands were moving and by watching them I began to perceive lines of energetic fibers flowing from her fingertips. I began to follow the lines and heard a beautiful melody coming from a flute in the distance.

Sitting quietly I closed my eyes and danced along the lines of awareness feeling a sense of immense peace emanating from my being. The Earth began to pulse in a steady rhythmic beat and in a short time I pulsed harmoniously with her. Each beat seemed to widen the area in which we were sitting until it felt as though we were simply floating in the vastness of the Earth's emanations.

The *voice of Seeing* began, a silent knowing that was emerging and aligning with my being: "Humanity has forgotten their origin and has become deeply distracted by so many external influences and far-fetched concepts. Even those who are attempting to reawaken have become preoccupied with deceitful endeavors that continue to keep them at a great distance from the Lineage of all life on Earth."

I felt a tiny fire burn within my heart, and the burning sensation I experienced soon spread throughout my entire body. My mind and body felt so relaxed and I could not remember a time when I felt so free and unencumbered. Without opening my eyes I saw that El Cuervo was deeply aligned with the flow of energy that was flowing through and all around us. The woman appeared to be translucent, she was there but I could see through her, and an expansive energetic aura was effervescing all around her.

"The Lineage," the voice of Seeing continued, "is an ancient line of power, a flame that appeared instantaneously at the point of origin. I cannot tell you what it is; I can only tell you what it is not. For millions of years seers have dedicated their lives to keeping this flame alive. They work ceaselessly to strengthen their connection to the Earth, align with Source, and continuously learn from silent knowledge.

"These seers became known as warriors, those who fought and continue to fight fiercely to preserve the Lineage. The fight is not against others, as in warring nations or man-against-man and other Earthly inhabitants. It is a battle for the preservation of awareness, of the abstract, and the freedom to maintain a balanced connection to the harmonious and ephemeral nature of existence.

"Warriors know that life on Earth is in peril. Unlimited growth and consumption are causing a great imbalance, one that she may not recover from. The Earth is the epicenter of our being, the being on which we were born, and the being from which we will depart. Sadly, she has been ignored by too many for far too long, and if this negligence continues the flame will diminish and may eventually extinguish. Should the flame of awareness perish, the beings of the Earth will instantaneously cease to exist."

We returned to silence and I floated through the cosmos

looking down at the Earth. The entire planet was pulsing, and I could hear and perceive the totality of it. It had taken on a translucence that was similar to that of the Indian woman. I saw through to the center of the Earth and gazed at the ancient fire burning within her. At once I noticed three other tiny flames moving from the center and outwards onto the surface of the Earth. From each of those three fires several more fires moved outwards again, and from those even more. Soon there were tiny fires burning all over the Earth.

The feeling that washed over me while witnessing people sitting around the hearth, the sacred fire, was one of honor and reverence. A multitude of fibrous lines enveloped me that revealed equilibrium and synergy. I sensed a frequency, a tone that emanated from the Earth, and I knew without knowing that it was the vibration of the Earth which held all of her beings aligned to her and to each other.

I continued watching the burning fires, knowing that I am connected to a force that has existed for billions of years, when suddenly, the vibrational tone shifted, and I saw some of the fires going out. The peaceful feeling I just experienced was turning into one of sorrow, extreme sadness. The fires were not burning out, they were being extinguished by a different type of force; a force that sought to consume the fires of awareness.

I struggled to not cry out. I felt the flame within my own heart flicker and with that my own fight to keep it burning brightly. It could not die, would not! I looked down at the Earth again and was relieved to see that some fires continued to burn, but not many.

The voice of Seeing began again. "Balance is needed to keep the fires burning. Too many people have lost their connection to the Earth and are, instead, attached only to the machinations of their minds. This is a trap, one that keeps the body anchored in sensory identification aligned with the frequency of fear. Buried deep in the subconscious of humans resides the creative fluidity, harmony, and freedom of Spirit.

"Too much emphasis is placed upon the personal. The burning flame of Spirit, the purity, wholeness, and wisdom, are no longer fueled and are burning themselves out. Self-identity and Spirit must be brought back into balance through individuation. This will allow for an awakening of subconscious qualities. People will remember the nature of being human within the universe, this vast sea of awareness. They will remember why they projected themselves into human form upon the Earth in the first place."

I took all of this in, understanding through my own knowing that I had received from both Nayeli and inner silence. I began to think about the roots of a tree.

"Yes," the voice said. "The roots that grow in the Earth are the required energy for balance between mind and Spirit. The Earth nourishes and nurtures everything that is rooted and grounded upon her. If you dig up a plant, even if you are careful to dig a wide enough hole to get all of the roots, a slight bit of damage occurs as the roots foundational integrity is disrupted. As a result, the plant will go into shock and may either revive after being nurtured or it will wither and die. The same is true of animals. If you remove an animal from the wild, its connection to the Earth becomes severed and while it may continue to exist behind the bars that imprison it, its Spirit has been broken. It continues to exist within the confines to which it has been reassigned, in a lethargic manner devoid of Spirit."

"Humanity is experiencing this lethargy in increasing numbers. As people become more and more disconnected from their energy source of the Earth, they lose their ability to feel energetic, vibrant, and whole. As a result, they become passive, debilitated, and confused. These unhealthy qualities cause people to reside within a constant state of reason as they consistently attempt to rationalize their reality. No longer connected to the web of life, they begin to experience loneliness and fear. They often fall into a pattern of consumption that they hope will fill the void within. The fire within begins to weaken. This void will never be filled with material things, and the mind obsessively analyzes, dissects, and reviews the segments that make-up their lives. Rather than holding the awareness of unity through Spirit, they instead feel the impending doom of separation. It is at this point that the fires begin to fade and eventually burn out completely.

"Balance must be restored!" And then the voice was gone.

I began to cry after all I had perceived when suddenly I heard small children laughing. I abruptly opened my eyes to find that El Cuervo and I were sitting next to each other in the ruins. I looked for the Indian woman but did not see her anywhere. I got up and ran through the portals and up the stone steps. There wasn't a soul in sight. Going back into the ruins I stood in the doorway of the last T and asked, "El Cuervo? Were you there too?"

He said solemnly, "Yes, Nubecita, I saw the tyranny of the world in its attempt to extinguish the natural order and flow of awareness."

"Who was that lady, was she real?" I asked.

"As near as I could tell, she was as real as you or I," he said.

"What did she do to us? It was as though we were transported into the universe to see the origination point of the Earth. Did you see the fire burning from within the Earth?" I asked.

"I saw that and all of the fires becoming extinguished," he said. "I saw the potential that humanity has to fuel those fires so that they may begin, once again, to feel unified on this planet as the creator beings that they came here to be. It is very sad to see so much separation from Spirit and the desolation that follows."

"At first I saw horrible things," I said. "It started when we were given the example of the animals becoming imprisoned. I saw them sitting in cages in zoos becoming completely domesticated and how separation from the Earth leads them to devastating lives filled with fear and distress. Then I saw how humans have also become domesticated, how they too live with fear and distress and how, as their fires begin to dwindle, they lose hope and become susceptible to despondency and disease."

We sat quietly, each mulling over our own thoughts for a while. "But then, I could see the potential too," I added. "It was a slow process, an evolutionary process. People began to remember the importance of unity. This ignited the fires within them, just a little at first. And then, through that unity, they realized feelings of peace, and the flames expanded a little bit more, and their minds became less cluttered. Their minds began to move from the imprisonment that it had been taught to perceive, and they moved, one by one, onto the Earth, breathing her essence into their being. The fires were fanned through this breath and began to burn brightly again. And then, like a natural phenomenon, the people lost their obsession with their minds. They were able to see the glow of awareness as they remembered the source energy that is grounded in the Earth. They become effervescent fibrous lines of awareness, their emanations spreading and sparking remembrance into every cell of their bodies. And then, in a heightened state of attention, they began to burn with the fire from within, remembering that they are the universal life-force energy that flows in unity and without separation throughout the cosmos!"

I sat back against the wall of the ruins exhausted and spent. I began to cry a little, partly out of sadness and partly out of the hope that this vision would one day soon become a reality. El Cuervo came over and sat down beside me, holding me in his arms.

"That was, by far, one of your most beautiful dances in awareness," he said. "Thank you for your commitment, for your ability to see the brilliance of the universe so fully. There is no doubt in my mind that as your own emanations continue to align with the emanations of Spirit, with the entire universe, that you will dance effortlessly, in total freedom, throughout eternity."

Bands of Awareness

A shift of perception allows one to see that all of creation throughout the universe emerges from pure consciousness. Without consciousness, nothing would exist.
- Nayeli

When I awoke the next morning after a restful night's sleep, I looked out of my tent and saw El Cuervo sitting under a mesquite tree with his eyes closed. He looked serenely beautiful, almost like the Buddha meditating under the Bodhi tree.

Thinking back to the previous day's experience, I realized that we were both given the opportunity to see the promise of freedom for the Earth and all her inhabitants. Each fire within every person emitting energy outwards into the world as a means of keeping precious life-force energy flowing.

"Where to today, Nubecita?" he asked when he noticed me watching him as he sat under the tree. It was just like him to proceed to the next moment. We hadn't really discussed what had happened inside of the ruins with the young Indian woman. We had both been too immersed in our own thoughts to attempt to put the event into the trappings of reason.

I asked him what he thought about going to Durango, Colorado since we were so close. I hadn't been there for several years and yearned for a lush green environment with all its moisture and coolness. We drove until we reached Farmington, New Mexico, and stopped for a quick breakfast. In less than an hour, we drove from an expanse of dry yellow desert to deep green ponderosa pines.

On the outskirts of Durango, El Cuervo turned down a dirt road, and we traveled through a canyon along the beautiful La Plata River. We found a clearing near the river that was not part of a designated camping area and set up our tents. When I finished I sat at the edge of the river, put my feet in and pulled them out quickly, gasping at how cold the water was.

After a while I settled down and let the river take away the excitement and anticipation that I had been carrying inside me since we left Mexico. I attempted to allow my mind to clear, but from years of experiencing the quiet of the desert, I found the forest to be incredibly noisy. The river was loud, the birds were louder, and I swear that I could hear the plants growing. At times it seemed that I actually watched vines move, fern tendrils unfold, and flowers open. Animals appeared all around; ground squirrels, chipmunks, salamanders, deer, raccoon, rabbits, startling me continually. Even the rustle of the leaves from a breeze blowing through the canopy of the trees along the river's edge unnerved me at first. Soon, however, it became a sound I enjoyed immensely.

Heightened awareness proved to be very different in the forest. In the desert when I would enter into heightened states of awareness, it was rare for me to feel grounded. Nayeli had explained this to me saying that while the desert oozes power, we can grab onto those lines and dance along them. The forest, on the other hand, pulls power into the Earth.

I became a little agitated that it was taking me so long to

become still and was relieved when El Cuervo, who was sitting somewhere back from the river near the tents, started to drum. I focused on the slow, rhythmic beat of the drum and began to feel the familiar pulse of the Earth and hear her heartbeat.

Relaxing more deeply, I blended in with my surroundings, no longer aware of whether El Cuervo was still drumming. I recalled my response to Nayeli's statement about recapitulating the stories of the Earth. "Why would I want to do that Nayeli?" I had asked, reminding her how much I disliked the stories. With much resolve she had stated simply, "Because you are a woman and you can. When you immerse yourself into the body of the Earth you come to know what she has been holding, and then the stories of the world as we know them today begin to make sense. The stories that reveal themselves to you are energetic lines that can be traced back to their inception. You will come to know the patterns that humanity has become bound by, and then you can begin the arduous yet rewarding task of recapitulating them."

"What!" I exclaimed. "What could possibly be rewarding about it? Recapitulating patterns that don't even belong to me? How does any of this make sense!"

I recalled Nayeli's laugh as she explained to me that a warrior's goal is to unite with the awareness of the Earth in order to have the energy necessary to align with or even assemble a new band of awareness. "Alignment has to be very peaceful and very fluid. If you don't recapitulate the patterns of the Earth before you align with her emanations, they will persist within your energy body as a sort of anchor. No matter what band you align with or assemble, those patterns will always remain ingrained.

"Furthermore," she continued, "you may not even be able to align with a new band of awareness if you are still attached to any of the stories that are exclusive to humans on Earth. You have to connect with the Earth on a very deep level in order to restore that sense of reverence that was once held by all people for her. Not everyone understands that she is a living sentient being. By connecting with her deeply you will come to know her through what you will see and sense and feel from her. In this knowing you will come to understand that your final boost will come from her, the boost that will energize you so fully that you will be able to align with her emanations and enter into a new band of awareness."

While I did not understand everything Nayeli had been telling me, for as long as I had known her I knew that I could trust her with my life. She never steered me in a direction that was not conducive to my path of freedom and never presented me with any challenges that I could not overcome. Nayeli didn't just guide me, she empowered me to make the choices that were necessary for me to expand my wisdom and awareness without pressuring me to do so. She did it in a way that made sense to me as opposed to following some articulated lesson plan that she had formulated. Her awareness, compassion and fluidity are traits that I admire. Seeing what became possible for her is what compels me to constantly gather power and continually push the boundaries of perception.

I learned that the band of awareness she speaks of is the ability that we have to assemble and create new realities by simply aligning with the emanations of the Earth. I saw these emanations while sitting in the ruins with El Cuervo.

"What are these emanations?" I had asked her.

"They are the force of power, the fibrous lines that lie within reach of our fingertips. They are the indescribable commands that are awaiting their creation through our intention. They are a masterpiece, a manifestation of beauty just as we, ourselves, have become manifest through intention alone," she had answered.

When our awareness is aligned with other energetic forces, including the Earth, great and amazing things become manifest. This is a result of what is perceived by the awareness that is doing the perceiving.

We are a feeling, a mood, a sensation devoid of thought; consciousness randomly floating throughout the universe aligning with other emanations within the universe. Merging with them and becoming something more than nothing. Becoming aware from the sheer force of perceiving in tangent with Source itself and in that awareness all things become possible and true.

If we are able to recognize creative Source energy for what it truly is, then all we need to know is that creation is a matter of will. It is within our innate ability, with determination and fortitude, to align with the emanations at large to bring something into existence. We are the manifestors and the creators of our realities. We created our very existence into this realm of human form.

When we consider that all of the planets and stars are manifestations of an intention as an act of creation, we begin to realize that our power to create is unlimited. The Earth did not just take form as a planet and stop there; she created herself and the many things upon her as part of her creation. What joy and delight, to constantly weave a magical tapestry of beauty in balance and harmony, without limitations. Fueled by the inexhaustible well of Source energy, the Earth continues her spectacular and miraculous dance, ever present and constantly evolving.

The Earth doesn't think about anything, she just creates. She is an amazing teacher who reminds us that as creators and co-creators, we can let our consciousness interact. We can dance with the fields of energy that lie at the center of consciousness within us. All we have to do is surrender and trust with the totality of our hearts and our souls; to let our passions take over and lead us in the magnificent dance with all of creation. And herein lies our ability to create a new band of awareness in which to reside, anywhere we'd like within the cosmos.

The bottom line, Nayeli had told me, is that we created ourselves to be here, in human form, on this beautiful Earth, here and now. All we have to do is connect with the pulse of the Earth. This brings us to fully know Source and helps us remember what the illusory world has taught us to forget.

One day, she had suggested that I consider *una búsqueda del silencio*.

"La búsqueda del silencio?" I asked. "You mean like a vision quest?"

"No, not a vision quest. A pursuit; a search for silence" she said. "You are not seeking vision, what you are seeking is a connection with silence; deep, profound silence through which you may very likely receive visions. Sitting in silence helps your intuition to broaden beyond your individual consciousness thereby increasing your perception and understanding. New awareness comes from silence, often revealing information that you had no previous exposure.

She explained, "La búsqueda is an amazing commitment

that will gently guide you outside of your comfort zone and effectively shift your assemblage point. La búsqueda will provide you with fresh perspective and allow you to perceive in a new way. This will help you to connect intimately and deeply with the Earth and the mystery of Source energy. Every culture around the planet has performed a quest of this nature."

She told me that in order to do this I had to first identify the place in which I would like to sit and to make sure it's a comfortable place where I will feel secure and relaxed because it would be best to stay there for many hours, perhaps overnight. Once I selected the place, I should begin a cleanse by eliminating my limited intake of meat entirely and to eat only fresh fruit, vegetables and grains for at least five days prior. I really love coffee so when she mentioned that I should drink tea and water instead, I panicked. The more I thought about it though, the more I realized that I had been long overdue for a cleanse and actually looked forward to it.

"Sitting upon the Earth is the most powerful teacher and catalyst," Nayeli said. "In current times the connection to nature has become vastly diminished. This connection was such an integral part of Spiritual, emotional, and physical vitality for our ancestors and it is time for you to learn how to listen to inner voices and truths. You will come to know the pulse of the Earth and through this pulse you will align with Source and silent knowledge.

"When sitting upon the Earth in stillness, silence replaces the bombardment of words that have always shaped and formed our realities. We begin to become aware in a new way. The sounds of the Earth coax us into listening, and a new form of conscious awareness opens within us. It is from within this silence that we come to hear the true nature of the desert or forest or oceans without naming them. It affords us the opportunity to perceive the energies that bring form onto this planet. We hear in a way we have never heard before, sounds emerge from a living planet that have the potential to make us laugh and smile and appreciate the awesome beauty in which we have the privilege of residing."

What she described filled me with a longing to sharpen my senses and perceive energy on a new level. I eagerly anticipated deepening my connection with the Earth and Source by strongly considering her advice to engage in la búsqueda.

"As we continue in this practice of silence and gratitude upon the Earth," she went on, "we arrive at a state of humility, respect, and wonder. We are moved to witness, intuit, and know the deep connection that we each have with everything within the entire web of life. Our gift for recognizing that we are but a mere piece of an enormous living whole comes through us in the form of knowledge and greater still, wisdom. We begin to recognize that to trust and surrender and to be in the flow is the only way to exist. Once our vibrational frequency has increased, our awareness becomes heightened, and we come to know that the only choice we have is to live authentically. The only dream we have is the dream of the planet; the dream of the universe. And the only reality that energizes us is the one in which we are creators and co-creators."

What she had told me fascinated me and I began to anticipate my quest. Intrigued by the pulse of the Earth I asked her to tell me more about it. She elaborated by saying, "Since the beginning of its creation the Earth has had a pulse of life to which every living organism is connected. This pulse has surrounded and protected all living beings with a natural frequency vibration. It is like a heartbeat that unifies everything in a diverse and interdependent web of creation."

"The Earth," she continued, "resonates at a frequency that correlates with the average frequency of alpha brain waves in human beings. If our bodies are deprived from natural exposure to these frequencies, we are less likely to live in a state of wellness and will become out of balance with the electromagnetic vibrational frequencies of the Earth. And if we vibrate at a lower frequency than that of the surrounding frequencies, we become dense and heavy. We begin to feel as though we are dragging ourselves through life with a lot of resistance, feeling as though we are under pressure. We feel this way because we *are* under pressure. It is the basic law of physics. If we are not aligned with the energetic frequency of the Earth and Source, we have essentially increased our body mass, which increases its density. It's no wonder so many people feel lethargic and fearful. They are not in equilibrium with the external vibrational frequency pressure that is surrounding them."

This was a lot to consider, and my brain was working in overdrive to make all of the connections.

"Relax," she said as if reading my thoughts, "everything will make more sense to you once you are on the land actually having the experience. You cannot attempt to rationalize that which you do not yet know."

"So," I said, "you are basically saying that when we sit on the Earth, we become grounded in our root chakra and are better able to successfully open and clear all of our other chakras through which the flow of unobstructed energy can move continuously through us, right?"

She had nodded in agreement adding, "This allows us to be energetically nourished and whole which in turn ensures that our vibrational frequencies are rhythmically in sync with everyone and everything around us. This is when we are able to fully be in the natural flow of life in order to live within the moment.

"Sitting upon the Earth and connecting with the pulse of the Earth helps us to restore our vibrational frequency and achieve equilibrium. When we attain this kind of balance, we have a natural tendency to become still and silent. It is within the silence that the distractions of our lives decrease enough to allow us to begin to make sense of the world. This helps us to recognize the simplicity of our natural existence."

"What should I bring with me on this search for silence, and how long will I be there?" I asked.

"Just bring yourself, and make sure you have enough layers of clothing to keep yourself warm. You may bring a blanket or sleeping bag if you'd like and a bottle of water but don't bring any food with you and for this search of silence, don't bring a journal, iPod or phone," she said. "You don't want any distractions. You can bring some matches if you want in case you decide to spend the night and want to start a fire. Give yourself a couple of days to organize your thoughts."

As I sat by the river considering all that Nayeli had told me about la búsqueda, and in light of the events that had unfolded with the Indian woman at Chaco Canyon, I began to anticipate, with excitement, that perhaps I should begin to prepare myself to undertake this task as soon as possible.

Habitual Patterns and Thought Forms

Patterns are maintained by consistently giving energy to a system of power. I choose freedom from the routines, from the patterns, from the human collective. My life is about walking each moment in full awareness, forever touching it, honing it, and knowing it through the grandeur that is our existence here upon this earth.
- El Cuervo

I phoned Nayeli from Durango to check in with her and she asked if I had gone on la búsqueda yet. I told her I hadn't but was preparing for it and would be going within the next day or two. She was excited to hear all the news of our travels to this point and couldn't wait for the next update.

El Cuervo's response to me, after I asked him what he felt was most important about la búsqueda was, "It's an opportunity to align with Source energy and from there, to take abstract ideas and make them real."

I mulled over this statement for a while then said, "That sounds kind of ambiguous. Would you care to expound a bit?"

He told me that if humanity were to evolve beyond the state of mental slavery to which they were bound, they would have to come up with some new ideas that would be beneficial to the beings of the planet. If they did not, they would just wind up doing the same things over and over again without positive results. "When we surrender to silent knowledge, we exist within a realm that is free of reason, and that which emerges from the abstract presents the potential for innovation and opportunity. People are afraid of the unfamiliar and rely, instead, on things that exist in the dominion of reason."

"Yeah," I quipped. Instead of implementing something new that could have a profound impact for all of humanity, everyone just complains about things the way they are and then repeat the patterns over and over again."

"Exactly. Take for example, that drum circle you attended a few years ago," he said. "Even though those people were attempting to work outside the box, they didn't introduce or create anything new, they simply repeated patterns. A trap of attention bolstered by self-importance and hierarchal absurdity."

The memory of the surreal event came back to me. I had gone to a mailing center to ship a package and noticed a flier posted that said:

Drum Circle

Prerequisite: You must know how to journey

I considered that a drum circle might be a fun experience, a change of pace; after all, that's what we often did in Mexico with Nayeli, Alejandro, and the other warriors. We journeyed into the unknown. We drummed, we danced, and we journeyed.

I pulled off a tab with a phone number and called when I got home. A woman with a breathy voice named Lakshmi or something like that answered, and then asked me if I knew how to journey. "Lakshmi," I said, "my life is a journey." She hesitated for a moment then with a forced laugh said, good answer. She gave me dates, times, and directions to her house.

I didn't know what to expect when I pulled up at her house in the dark and parked among other cars. I followed a gravel path up a hill to a yurt that was lit with candles and smelled like incense. An abalone shell was by the door with sage burning in it, and after removing my shoes and my denim jacket I smudged myself with the sage and timidly walked over to an empty spot on the floor with my drum.

People were talking and were wearing everything from decorated shawls to very unique and large jewelry, shells, feathers, beads, hats, and I remember a lot of velvet. The men too! One guy had a hat on that resembled a coyote head, and he wore a very large quartz crystal around his neck. I watched in rapt attention as more and more people filed into the yurt. I created a vacuum of invisibility around me, one of the things a warrior brother taught me. "Pull in all of your energy and hold it within the confines of your physical body. This way, no one will be able to detect you if they are not a seer."

Suddenly, the man with the coyote hat beat his drum loudly three times and called the circle to order. Everyone took their place seated on the floor. He welcomed everyone and said that the intention for the evening was a group healing session and to begin, we would all stand up and call in the directions. I watched what everyone else did so I would be able to emulate them and not look too out of place.

We faced the east as a woman had been delegated to call in that direction. "Spirits and energies of the east," she said loudly in a deep and resonant voice. Everyone was holding their palms turned upright as we faced the east so I did too. "Come to be with us this evening, to guide us into illumination and help us to see each moment as a new beginning. Aho." And everyone echoed that word 'Aho.' In Spanish, the word ajo, means garlic, and I wondered if we were calling upon garlic to ward off evil spirits or vampires. The session continued with a different person within the circle calling in each of the directions which included mother Earth, father sky, and the great mystery.

I didn't understand why the energies were called in to the circle because I had come to know that we are surrounded by each of them in all moments. Nayeli and Alejandro refer to the different directions as winds that are associated with specific energy centers. They taught me that the winds represent power and to enter into a state of gratitude whenever they approach. In addition, we are to be mindful of the direction from which the wind blows to ensure our connection with it, as well as the opportunity it provides for us to receive the messages it brings to us. The winds deliver power into our bodies and serve as gateways into higher awareness.

This ritualistic behavior that I witnessed in the yurt intrigued me greatly since the warriors I know never did any formalized ceremonies. They had explained to me that while ritual has the power to move one's attention away from self-absorption, it can adversely trap the attention by fixating the position of the assemblage point. Rituals that originated as a way to honor the flow of life had more often, over time, become empty and meaningless. Those conducting them often did so by rote as opposed to truly connecting with the flow of energy that they were attempting to call forth.

The next thing that happened was the coyote hat man who

held a stick covered in feathers, beads, crystals and bells told everyone how happy he was to have such a large turn-out. He said with a haughty tone, "my name is Coyote Man and my purpose is to trick Earthly humans into enlightenment. Aho." And everyone answered back "aho." Garlic I privately groaned.

The ornate stick went to the next person and the next and the next. There were a whole myriad of interesting names in that circle. Whistling Elk, Barbara Moonglow, High Flying Eagle, Rainbow Woman, John Walking Bear, Gaia, Sacred Heart. Each person also stated their credentials as certified shamans, certified soul retrievers, certified dreamworkers, certified extraction healers and more things that I can't remember. They had also stated their purpose and what their specific contribution to humanity was. I had felt very out of place and when the stick was handed to me I simply stated, Lorraine, my first name as given to me at birth and said, "Thank you for letting me be here tonight" quickly passing the stick.

When everyone had spoken Coyote Man said, "We will now drum to connect with the higher divine goddess power, to open ourselves to receive the healing we need, and the healing we can give. When we are finished we will begin the healing sessions. Whoever is in need of healing will have a chance to move to the center of the circle. Those who want to give healing will gather around those in the center. If you prefer you may drum or lie down on the floor and journey." I looked forward to the drumming, it had been a very long time since I had drummed.

A slow beat began and grew louder as more and more people drummed. It was a steady, monotonous beat, very unlike the energetic, organic, and vibrant beats that we played on our drums in Sonora. We drummed for a very long time until Coyote Man beat his drum very loudly in three successive beats, obviously indicating it was time to cease because everyone immediately stopped drumming. They were all breathing hard describing how altered they were and how powerful they had felt during the drumming.

Coyote Man then asked those who had been called to receive healing to please lie on the floor in the middle of the room. Next he asked for those who had been called to provide healing to surround the people on the floor. I sat and watched with several other people as those who wanted to receive healing moved towards the center of the room. Coyote Man politely asked those of us who were sitting on the edges to begin drumming, using a steady beat as we had done earlier. He called it a shaman's beat.

We started to drum and since there were fewer of us it wasn't as loud as before. Many of the people who were providing the healing had rattles and were shaking them in rhythm to the drum beats. In a very short period of time those who identified themselves as healers, danced wildly around the yurt. They screamed out animal noises and contorted their bodies in the oddest of ways over the people lying on the floor. What is this? I thought to myself. After having recently connected so deeply with silent knowledge in the company of Nayeli and Alejandro, this was sheer mayhem and a far cry from any of the healing that I had experienced from the curanderos in Mexico.

Once again the circle had quieted down and everyone returned to their places on the floor. As before, participants were breathing heavily while describing how altered they were and how powerful the experience had been. All were given the opportunity to share. What was disturbing to me was that as some recounted their journeys, they were never offered the opportunity or assistance to discover meaning. They were told by Coyote Man and some of the supposedly certified shaman that they carried deep wounds. They were told they could schedule an appointment with one of the certified healers at the end of the ceremony.

When the journey sharing had ended, we were instructed to stand again in order to release the energies of the directions that we had called in earlier. Soon thereafter everyone started hugging each other, talking, and networking. Healing sessions were scheduled. One overly friendly woman who had stared at me a lot during the evening, walked over to me and seemed interested in making small talk.

"I haven't seen you here before, are you new to the area?" she asked. "No," I told her, "but this is my first time to this circle." She asked me if I felt the power moving through the room during the healing session. Though I hadn't really felt anything I told her I did, it seemed to be what she wanted, needed, to hear. "So," she said, "are you a certified shaman?" I told her that I didn't even know that shaman required certification or that certifications were a necessity.

"Well," she boasted, "I have completed the arduous program of advanced shamanistic healing and have received the golden egg certification of completion that sanctions me to perform ritual, ceremony, and provide training. Would you like to sign up for a course? I have a new class starting soon. In fact, you can even take it online if you want."

"Uh, no thank you," I said trying to sound enthusiastic, "but I do sincerely appreciate the offer."

I mustered the courage to continue. "I do have a question I'd like to ask if you don't mind." She perked up and I could tell that she was the type of person that would have an answer to anything anyone asked. "Why," I began slowly, "do you say garlic at the end of each sentence shared in the circle?" "She looked at me, bewildered and said, "garlic? We don't say garlic." "Yes, in Spanish, the word for garlic is ajo and I notice that you all say it with much frequency. "Oh!" she said relieved, "aho! We say aho at the end of each statement for closure. It's a Native American word much like the word amen."

"All I can add, El Cuervo," after recalling this bizarre event, "is that these people reminded me of zombies. They were all trained to memorize some ridiculous rhetoric and perform it on each other. Now I understand why the seers are so opposed to ritual and why they believe that ritual only serves as a bombastic trap of attention. Not a drop of creativity existed in that room, just a bunch of self-important people who performed for each other."

The irony of it, as I later found out, is that many of the ritualistic components demonstrated that evening were, indeed, at one time integral ceremonial aspects held by various tribes throughout the world. El Cuervo explained to me that the word Aho actually means much more than amen, but that people who are intent on sounding as though they contain deep knowledge are merely repeating words without knowing their true meaning. Aho, he said, is more like a confirmation to the Great Spirit that expresses the fact that the words spoken by an individual already exist in an act of co-creation with Spirit.

Someone along the way who had studied tribal societies decided to concoct a certification course. The sad thing about it was that the lack of innovation and new vision. What had been started long ago as a beautiful tradition to specific tribal people had become a ritualized pattern devoid of meaning. A true shaman probably brought an idea from the abstract and put it into form for his tribe. Wrought with meaning for their specific needs it had become, all these years later, packaged as a commodity for consumption and reduced to a hollow certification course.

As Nayeli had explained to me, this drum circle and other events I have experienced throughout my life have provided me with the opportunity to come to know all of the stories of man from a point of awareness. She has stressed repeatedly to avoid attaching to any of them through approval or disdain.

"In knowing the stories," she added, "you will see the energetic fibers and lines that are rooted to a single point. When you see that point, and only when you see it, you will recognize it as the point of origin from which all patterns flow, and that is the point that you must recapitulate. They are the stories of the Earth, of humanity, and each time a pattern is recapitulated, your assemblage point will move again."

"The path of the warrior," said El Cuervo interrupting my thoughts of Nayeli, "isn't for everyone even though ordinary man consistently searches to fill the holes with something of substance. What they don't seem to realize is that the things they so desperately seek to fill the empty spaces doesn't come from another person's story or from a world of objects. It comes from allowing the emptiness to flow through them. It is from being empty that we are constantly filled. This is what you stand to gain from la búsqueda, the opportunity to become empty so you can connect with silent knowledge."

Everywhere my journeys took me, the stories were the same. Emphasis was rarely placed on connecting with silence or perceiving something new. Creative empowerment was not being offered as a viable option towards self-discovery. What I witnessed were present day people attempting to embody things of the past and to excel at them. People were determined to allow their assemblage points to remain fixated upon outmoded stories, even in their struggle to be free.

Most disturbing to witness had been the competitive battle between people to be bigger, better, more powerful, and more knowledgeable than others as they each vied for positions of false power by engaging in the trivial and haughty spectacle of one-upmanship. A pattern that repeats itself where no one is exempt except those who choose not to participate.

The powerful feeding on the meek so they may bolster their own self-importance. The meek striving for something more while the powerful halt their potential, sometimes under the guise of compassion. Keeping them ever so meek and dependent through the constant talk of love with so little of it actually being shared was maddening.

Nayeli told me one day that people, through their feelings of inadequacy, isolation, and separation, fight each other in their attempt to feel more important and powerful. "How very sad," she said, "that they do this to each other. Can you imagine how incredible the world would be if instead of fighting one another they gave each other support and guidance? They would come to find that by empowering each other, how very powerful they could be and how many things they could create with ease."

Nayeli was right. Homogenous people all over the world are striving for equality and unification while chanting the mantra of one-mind in their quest for the ultimate truth. They are completely willing to relinquish their individuality for the sake of belonging yet never come to realize that the very thing they seek lies within them.

I began to see through the stories and into the patterns of the stories. I came to recognize that these patterns had been upheld for a very long time. I even caught glimpses of how they came to be. Seeing the point of origin and the natural flow of Source energy becoming corrupted seemed unreal to me.

I know that a warrior doesn't indulge in emotions but I also know that a warrior has the ability to feel each emotion in its totality. I remember a warrior sister saying, "I am so grateful for even small emotional pain these days. Each revelation allows a penetration of awareness which encompasses the inner hole to reveal emptiness. If you stay with the emptiness, you discover space. If you stay with the space, you begin to reclaim your lost essence."

The Changing Face of the Shaman

I don't care how many people want to call themselves shaman, or how many people want to teach others some specific way to exist in life. These are patterns! What I am interested in is that people remain curious and enthralled by the advancement of knowledge and awareness from an evolutionary level and not from an intellectual one.

- Alejandro

After a wonderful evening along the edge of the La Plata River filled with personal recollection and revelation, El Cuervo and I packed our gear. It was early morning, and we decided to head towards Canyonlands, Utah, to enjoy some of the red rock beauty and explore the petroglyphs found throughout the area. Though it would add several hours to our destination, El Cuervo suggested that we take the southern loop so we could go through Monument Valley.

"I think that visiting Monument Valley prior to you embarking on la búsqueda will provide you with energy and balance" he said.

"Well that sounds good. But why will it help me with those things?" I asked, always curious to understand the workings of his mind.

"The Navajo have a legend about Changing Woman, and I

just feel that the energies of her story will invigorate you and provide you with insights that will be instrumental for your journey into silence," he said thoughtfully.

El Cuervo has always been very interested in creation folklore and traditional stories because he knows that each story originated from a universal truth. He has the uncanny ability for remembering stories and interpreting their meaning. It was no accident that his task was to reveal the common link that lie at the root of all paradigms because he certainly has the mind for such an undertaking.

"Tell me about the story, I'd love to hear it," I said knowing that whatever he shared with me would be valuable in expanding and my awareness.

"Changing Woman," he began, "represents the Earth and her life-giving qualities while in a continual state of movement and creative change. It is said that she ages through the seasons, only to become young once again to repeat the process with the changing of seasons. She loved the summer and the sun, and it is said that she lay naked upon a rock at the water's edge under the warmth of the sun. She opened herself to the warmth of the sun and found herself impregnated within days. She gave birth to twin boys named Sa'ah Naagháí and Bik'eh Hózhó. There are many versions of this story and some say that she gave birth to a boy named Sa'ah Naagháí and a girl named Bik'eh Hózhó, the son and daughter of Earth and sky."

My feet up on the dashboard and my seat reclined a little, I felt dreamy and content. The sun came in through the window to warm my face as I enjoyed El Cuervo's melodic voice recount the story.

"The twins were considered hero twins, their goal to

conquer the monsters of the Earth and to dispel illusion. However, Changing Woman told them to leave everything as it was so that humans who incarnated on Earth would be put to the test of remembering their source. 'It is through the challenges and the distractions, she explained to her children, that people can become strong warriors and effective in increasing their awareness.'"

"As a creator being, Changing Woman went on to create people, animals, vegetation, and other things that came to associate her with beauty and fertility. She symbolized the creation that comes from the union between elements of the cosmos, Earth and sun, or as some refer to them, mother Earth and Father Sun. Together she and her mate, the sun, were the embodiment of the relationship that people have with the Earth and her creatures, in balance and harmony. Sa'ah Naagháí Bik'eh Hózhó has powerful meaning among the Navajo people and is said to be deeply rooted and revered in their culture."

"What does it mean?" I asked.

"It has been generally translated into English to mean long life and happiness. It is also known to mean, walk in balance and beauty or to walk the beauty way. The beauty way is to walk in honor, appreciation, and gratitude for the Earth, all of her beings and elements. But for the Navajo, it is a profound philosophical part of their lives that applies to the very foundation of their existence. It represents that they are a piece of the greater whole of creation and that they are here to walk in balance and harmony with each other throughout their time on Earth and into eternity.

"It is also said that Sa'ah Naagháí means to walk gently upon the Earth with gratitude and respect so that you may grow to be content and fulfilled at the end of life. Bik'eh Hózhó means to be aligned with Universe and the Earth, simultaneously, in balance, sacredness, and beauty."

After thinking about his explanation I said, "It sounds like Sa'ah Naagháí Bik'eh Hózhó can be construed to mean that we are children of the universe and are all interconnected within the great web of all life. We must acknowledge that our lives are a gift and aspire to be on the same harmonious frequency of the flow of source energy at all times, with our entire environment. To walk in beauty we must be beauty."

"In a nutshell," he said.

I reflected on all aspects of this story, the metaphor and the similarities between many of the creation myths I had heard. They all seemed to originate from the same point. "El Cuervo?" I asked. "Of all the creation stories you know, what do you perceive as the common link at the center of all paradigms?"

"The acknowledgement of awareness," he immediately replied. "Each culture adapts the story in order to maintain the position of their assemblage point, and they continue to justify that position by retelling the story over and over. Eventually, the original point of awareness becomes lost within the repetitive dogma of the story, and people only come to know the details of the story instead of knowing that they exist as the actual energy of awareness.

"My belief in the whole thing is that the very first tribe or clan of humans to exist on Earth were completely aligned with awareness, with the wisdom of the cosmos, and the knowledge that their journey here was a transitory one. Over time, however, the tribe grew as more and more awareness incarnated on this Earth causing the tribe to scatter and spread. The true awareness of original source energy was only retained through the story. Over the course of thousands upon thousands of years, the connection to the original point of awareness was no longer accessible because mankind became more immersed in the world of reason."

"So they forgot that they were part of the original awareness that resides in the cosmos?" I asked.

"That's basically what I perceive and have come to know. There were shaman that lived within each tribe. These were men and women of power who had the ability to connect energetically to the source energy of the universe. All people have this ability but it was the shaman who remembered, who had maintained that connection of awareness. The role of the shaman was to remind everyone of the power that they each have within themselves. To be able to exist within the eternal connection of the oneness they have with Source. To recognize the center of consciousness, within themselves, so that they would no longer have to rely on anything except the wisdom of the universe."

"Are there still shaman?" I queried.

"There are shaman everywhere, and as more and more people awaken to the higher consciousness within them, the shaman emerges. Everyone is called, and everyone is chosen. All they have to do is be willing to explore what lies beyond their scope of conventional knowledge, the limited knowledge that has been instilled into humanity since birth. But few have the energy to leave the familiar behind so that they may leap into the silent knowledge that lies within the mystery."

"It seems to me," I interjected, "that more and more

people are beginning to question reality and are becoming willing to take that leap into the abyss of the unknown."

"This is true. Some are realizing that they are no longer content to take things at face value. They are no longer willing to accept the words and knowledge from quasi shaman or self-proclaimed gurus who claim to hold the key to freedom."

"What they yearn for," I said, "is to come to know the mystery in their own way, to explore and feel and sense their existence in the manner with which they resonate."

We remained silent for a while reviewing the conversation in our minds.

Eventually El Cuervo interrupted the silence: "What the *nuevos videntes,* or new seers and shaman hope to achieve is the opportunity to empower beneficiaries to access the knowledge and awareness that permeates the universe. To release the myth of man so that they can come to know the limitless potential that lies at the fingertips of those who dare to create their reality. Living life through the reality of a man-made myth serves no one.

"A true Shaman knows," he continued, "that the only one who can truly teach us awareness and wisdom is ourselves. As such, the shaman is there not to tell us how we should live our lives or conduct ourselves, but rather to encourage and empower us to connect to the mystery of life through all of our senses in order to create our own reality."

"Like Nayeli and Alejandro," I said, "They never tell us to do anything other than open ourselves to silence. Well," I considered, "they do tell us to recapitulate, and they assign us tasks."

"Yes, they do indeed," he said and we both laughed. "The

difference with Nayeli and Alejandro is that they are not telling us how to perceive or how to live. They don't tell us that we have to give up our Earthly possessions or live in celibacy or pay them money. They don't dangle carrots of promise in front of us or any of the hundreds of other things that pseudo-shaman and bogus gurus tell their apprentices. They provide us with the tools that are necessary for gaining the energy needed in order to relinquish the stories that have a hold over us. They know, through their own commitment and experience, the very things that prevent people from perceiving the world in a manner that is exceptional and pure."

"So true," I said. "I think of Nayeli as an empty mirror. She will do nothing more than stand before me, and the next thing I know, something shifts, and I recognize a piece of forgotten conscious awareness."

"Yes, we all mirror each other. The things that we don't typically like in others are often times the things that we don't particularly care for in ourselves. When it is mirrored to us, we can take accountability and release that reflection," he replied.

"I understand what you're saying," I said, "but it's more than that; Nayeli doesn't simply mirror me. She is an empty mirror and reflects nothing, or," I stopped, pausing to find the right words, "nothingness; emptiness. What I see swirling in Nayeli, in that pool of emptiness that she emanates, is the reminder of what lies beyond the reality of form. I am moved from my mind and into the center of my being, free from collective consciousness and into a place beyond time.

"In such moments, I feel as though every cell in my body is swirling and pulsating. I feel my body as it begins to vibrate and align with a resonate and harmonic frequency in the universe. My heart center expands, and as I breathe deeply into the center of my being, into the center of consciousness within me, I realize through my heart and not my mind that I am one with all things, no longer separate or containing an identity. My emanations merge and fuse with the emanations of the universe, and I feel at peace and at one with all. And when I return from this emptiness I am able to remember, with my whole body, that I am more than just a person and absolutely nothing at the same time. And then I say to Nayeli, 'What the heck did you just do to me?'"

"What does she say?" he asked inquisitively.

Giggling, I said, "she just laughs. And then, she'll say something like 'I didn't do anything. I simply aligned with the beauty of the universe so that you are able to see your own beauty within it."

"Wow, that's powerful. I like the concept of an empty mirror. It kind of sounds as though she becomes a portal," he said.

"You know, that's exactly what she becomes. She becomes like a gateway to the universe, to a place where all things are possible. In these moments I remember with clarity that we are all creator beings, that we created ourselves into human form so that we could acquire the awareness of being through our senses. I once told her that I wanted to stay in that place forever. She told me that eternity is a long time, and that one day I would return to it. She has always encouraged me to integrate everything I witness that exists beyond time and space into a state of higher consciousness so that I can become awareness itself. There is no reason, she has said, to allow ourselves to become so enmeshed in the stories of the Earth that we forget our point of origin."

"What's incredible, Nubecita," El Cuervo interrupted, "is that Nayeli has empowered you to completely transform, to become a changing woman who walks in beauty."

What he said was powerful to me and I looked forward to my quest for silence while surrounded by the beauty of the Earth. I recalled a beautiful Navajo prayer about the beauty way that I once read, and that impacted me greatly.

It begins in beauty.
In beauty may I walk;
All day long may I walk;
Through the returning seasons may I walk.

On the trail marked with pollen may I walk;
With grasshoppers about my feet may I walk;
With dew around my feet may I walk.

With beauty before me may I walk
With beauty behind me may I walk
With beauty above me may I walk
With beauty all around me,
may I walk.

In old age, wandering on a trail of beauty, lively;
In old age, wandering on a trail of beauty, living again.
It is finished in beauty.

- Anonymous

Merging with the Earth

The great silence of the earth allows one to merge effortlessly with trees and rocks. The silence, void of distractions, teaches one how to be fluid like water. It allows you to know the resounding pulse of the Earth as it resonates through your very being and shows you how to dance through the cosmos, so you can witness the eternal sunrises and sunsets as the earth continues to spin.
- Nayeli

It was a beautiful sunny morning, and the ground was steaming after a brief downpour had drenched the desert in the red rocks of the Canyonlands where we had set up camp the day before. A lot of great conversation, increased attention, and heightened awareness energized us exponentially after our journey throughout the four corners region.

I grew excited thinking about all the magical places we had explored and wondered where la búsqueda would unfold. One of my favorite places was a location in a low canyon next to a spring fed creek. It was bordered by beautiful green trees and surrounded by red cliffs, but there were a lot of mosquitos there. I decided that they would be too distracting in my attempt to connect with silence. I finally decided to go to the top of a rocky knoll that overlooked many amazing formations of balanced rocks and natural stone arches. The idea of sitting above so much beauty while almost touching the sky exhilarated me.

It was mid-summer. The area was prone to thunder and lightning storms both with and without rain. I hoped for clear skies. I headed out wearing a pair of shorts and a tank top walking in my trusty and sturdy hiking sandals. El Cuervo remained with our two tents, cooler and pick-up. He knew the general area where I'd be sitting; we'd hiked there together the day before.

"I plan to be gone for a few days and nights," I told him as he approached me. He bade me well as we embraced and we both laughed easily when he said, "May The Source be with you."

Along with two water bottles, I carried a blanket and a small plastic tarp as Nayeli instructed. I also carried some matches in my pocket as well as some sage. In spite of the warriors resistance to practicing rituals, I became accustomed to smudging areas with sage as a way of bringing in a feeling of well-being and cleansing, plus I enjoyed the fragrance immensely.

As I hiked up the trail, I spotted a small herd of deer grazing in the lower canyon by the spring. I walked as silently as possible so as not to startle them. In unison, they all looked up towards my direction. I stood perfectly still wondering how they did that. Did I make a nearly imperceptible noise that alerted each of them simultaneously to my presence? Did my scent touch them all at once? No, I decided, they are the perfect example of beings aligned with Source. They perceived me approaching. I entered into their field of perception, and they were able to see me without eyes, they just knew. Within thirty seconds, sensing their safety, they returned to grazing.

I had become accustomed to living out of a tent for the past week and a half and worked earnestly to continually hone my awareness. Nayeli was accurate in saying that the Earth has so much to show me. My entire focus had been on aligning with Source, and suffice it to say it was constantly unfolding around me. I began to recognize Source as an energy, an intelligence, an aware creator with a consciousness of its own. It was more than something that one just connects with or intends. It was proving to be a living connection that exists between all things, all beings. Like the deer. They are aligned with Source, and through their alignment, they just know. Source reveals itself to be a force that holds everything within it. Unlike the beliefs of many people I had met throughout my life, I believed Source not as a divine entity somewhere out in the universe, but as a flow of energy that surges through and around the Earth and everything else in the universe. A great mystery.

Arriving to my destination, I cleared an area of stones and laid my blanket out. I set down my water bottles, then stretched my arms wide, touching the ground and reaching up to the sky. There were many birds singing and flying about in the dewy coolness of the early morning. Among them, hummingbirds, stellar jays, ravens, vultures, hawks, sparrows and even more that didn't reveal themselves. As I sat on my blanket smelling the moist Earth from the morning rain I noticed bees, ants, and butterflies flitting around me. In a very short period of time some chipmunks appeared and were very curious about me.

Lighting some sage I offered my gratitude to this Earth, to her beings, to Nayeli and the warriors, and to the path that had brought me to this moment. My awareness began to shift and at first the changes seemed subtle; it grew quiet while stillness silenced the internal chatter as I continued to express my gratitude. I surrendered to the beauty that surrounded me. As all grew quiet, I felt as though I actually became a part of my surroundings, becoming one with the Earth no longer a separate entity.

I thought of how life with the seers was a constant act of creation, looking forward and evolving. Being in this world of endless patterns and stories overwhelmed me, and I had to touch the silence in the void. I closed my eyes and heard Nayeli gently say, "Align with the Earth so she may receive and transform the energy that doesn't serve you. It's all energy. You don't have to carry it the way you received it. Move through it, and then release it." Yes. Recapitulation, I reminded myself, is essential.

It had been a couple of hours since I arrived and I drifted off into a meditative state without much effort. Relaxed and peaceful, I intended myself to connect more deeply with the Earth. Lying on my back staring up at a crisp, blue, cloudless sky I began to feel as though I sank a little into the Earth, as comfortable as a down feather cushion. Little ants crawled on my body. A butterfly had even landed on me for a while before flying off. I felt a deeper sense of peace than I had experienced in a long time.

Suddenly I became overwhelmed by the lack of connection people today have with the Earth and with fluidity. I turned over and lay on my stomach on the still damp Earth and wept softly. What is it, I wondered, that makes people remain so fixated on the patterns? Can't they see how destructive those archetypes can be?

I felt the intense love of Nayeli, family, and friends wash

over me and felt the power of the teachings that they so willingly and freely give me. They never try to have power over me or prevent me from evolving; in fact they treasure and honor my commitment. They support me and encourage me and love me deeply, and I missed them deeply.

After releasing my sadness to the Earth, I thanked her for taking the energy and for holding me through it. In the absence of people, the Earth was my dance partner. I danced on her and with her every day and was grateful for her silent and unwavering companionship. To punctuate that thought, I rose from the Earth with my feet planted firmly and my arms outstretched above me and I swayed with gratitude. Feeling connected and content, I sat again.

Silence was what was missing in the world. No one made room for silence, almost forbade it. When they weren't busy talking, people were processing or planning or judging or reasoning or thinking. Even in their meditations others were guiding them with noises, chants, mantras, rattles or drums. Not to mention televisions, iPods, internet, smart phones, and video games; each noisy distraction constantly bombarding the senses and filling in otherwise empty spaces.

Quite close to me I suddenly heard a few pebbles roll and a puffing sound. I turned my head slowly to the direction of the noise to notice a small deer, a fawn, still with spots staring at me from a few feet away. "Align with Source!" I silently told myself. I brought this command deep into my heart and after the fawn circled for a couple of minutes, I pushed the energy of it into my womb, feeling the intense power of creation arise within me. The fawn, moving very slowly, came closer. I reaffirmed in my mind that I had aligned with Source and was experiencing the oneness of the moment.

I had no way of fully expressing myself, but I wished for you, and here you are. These words came from my heart as the deer continued to approach me. When judgment is fully suspended, and the seer acquiesces to silent knowledge, the dance with Source is infinite. I knew I had achieved a heightened state of awareness as I lay perfectly still, barely breathing. It put its nose into my hair and nudged me. I continued to just sit there giving gratitude to Source energy, to mother Earth, to the little fawn at my side. Then she turned and slowly walked away.

As I continued to sit there, I felt that I must surely be shining with what the warriors referred to as the *afterglow*, a luminescence that remains around the physical body after something extraordinary has occurred through a major shift in the assemblage point or state of heightened awareness. The feelings that arise in these instances are impossible to describe and have to be experienced directly. They have to be felt in order to fully know the totality of wonder and awe. The result from an awesome experience such as this is absolute fulfillment, joy, and success. This is what I felt. I joyfully succeeded in aligning with Source and felt very fulfilled. I knew for certain that if a satellite was flying over me in the sky, it would detect an unidentifiable glow on the Earth, a glow that was me, far below it.

I thought about Nayeli and sent her my gratitude, again, for this wondrous journey that she encourage me to take. I realized now that I became very dependent upon my fellow warriors, striving to attain the experiences that they had while pushing myself to do the things that they do, often in the way that they do them. It occurred to me that I had relied upon others to lead the way, and in so doing I had compromised my own ability of intuiting and connecting with my own intuition and creativity.

But I had become connected now and the moment that thought arose I felt and heard a light pulsing. I stopped breathing for a moment so that I could determine what it was, considering that my own heartbeat and pulse rate was rising, but it wasn't me. I felt very relaxed and quiet. Almost straining myself to hear the barely perceptible and steady rhythm, it became quite evident that I felt a very subtle and steady resonance beneath me. What could this be, I pondered as it grew delicately louder in its beat and tempo.

I realized then that everything, besides this steady pulse, had stopped. The birds were no longer singing, the breeze which had been gently blowing over me all day had ceased All was silent. Then I felt Nayeli's words wash over me. "You must honor the Earth at all times. She is our ultimate source and our greatest ally. It's important that you deepen your connection with her because it is she who will nurture you, protect you and energize you. You must connect with the pulse of the Earth, her very heartbeat itself." I was stunned.

Gradually I got the sensation of blending energetically with everything around me, including the heartbeat and pulse of the Earth. A song that a Mayan Shaman sang to me entered my mind, my being. *Tierra mi cuerpo, agua mi sangre, aire mi alimento, fuego mi espiritu.* Earth my body, water my blood, air my breath, and fire my Spirit. As it continued softly in the background, I felt and saw multitudes of energetic shimmering lines vibrating and sparkling brightly in front of me. I perceived these as the lines of the world, and they were beautiful in their iridescence and so hypnotic. I felt so invigorated, and though I didn't know exactly what they were, I moved towards them to dance among them.

Just at the moment of becoming absorbed into their glowing luminosity, I noticed a thick, dull line of energy that seemed to be lying still, not flowing buoyantly with the others. A strong feeling prompted me to follow it. The line had little brilliance and was flickering sporadically as though it were about to sputter out. Why, I wondered as I moved more deeply into the darkness along that line, was I urged to follow this one? It seemed like it was an obsolete line seldom used anymore.

Something caused me to suddenly awaken within this state of dream, this second attention, and I became very alert and conscious of my surroundings. A dream within a dream, but this was different. I have been here before though I knew it wasn't a past life or alternate reality. It was more like a remembrance of a place that I had been to, but not in a very long time.

I saw a weak fire flickering in the otherwise total blackness of this void, the luminosity of the other lines had disappeared. Where am I, I wondered?

I saw a fire that I intuited was the fire within the center of the Earth from which came all creation on this planet. The fire itself was started by a tiny spark from deep within the cosmos. A flame from this very fire lives within the form of all living beings. I began to perceive that what I witnessed was the origination point of Earthly consciousness and was instantly reminded of the Indian woman who we had encountered at Chaco Canyon.

I approached the fire, which seemed to be floating in mid-air and stood looking into it with awe at the immensity of the knowledge that I had just received. My brain didn't yet know how to make sense of the information.

The fire itself seemed to tell me that I had my own fire burning within me, and I am a very piece of infinity itself. There is no struggle to reach infinity when we are already a part of it. I crossed my legs, Indian style, and hovered buoyantly next to the fire. I wanted to put something on the fire to make it burn brighter, because it looked as though it was about to go out.

Just then it hit me that there is nothing that can be put on the fire to rekindle it. The fire depends on reciprocity in order for it to burn brightly. Not enough people are feeding the fire. It's coming to its end and will become extinguished soon.

I cried softly and said aloud, "The fire can't die. What will happen to us if the fire dies?" I saw deeply into the line I followed and knew that this was a line of antiquity, and infrequently used. The farther back I wandered on this line the more pure and vibrant it became.

I stopped and looked farther down the line into the darkness and perceived, from millions of years ago, the humans and animals and plant life that were connected to this line along with millions of beautiful little sparks of flame illuminating them. A captivating vibration emanated from the ancient depths of this line. I knew at that moment that it was the pulse of the Earth, harmoniously resonating with the flow of all things, with the universe, with Source.

I turned and looked back towards the direction from which I came and was surprised to see that there were far less fires burning there. I couldn't understand it, there were so many more people, so many more animals and yet, so few fires.

Overcome with exhaustion and confusion, I wrapped myself up in my blanket, tucked myself into a fetal position and began once again to cry.

I must have drifted off to sleep for a while, because as I opened my eyes, the leaves of a nearby tree were quivering in a gentle breeze producing a harmonious, natural song. Birds were singing, and the noises of this high desert had returned. I stood up feeling an energy coursing through me that seemed to awaken every cell within my body. I felt wholly connected to the entirety around me. Rocks, trees, animals, cactus, soil, sun. Everything in my body was moving, pulsing, and then I remembered the pulse of the Earth that had washed over me, moved around me and through me.

It was late afternoon. I decided to spend the night in this enchanting spot, which felt as though it was high above the Earth. I gathered dry leaves, small twigs and branches, preparing for the fire that I never built. As the sun began to set, the sky blazed in colors I hadn't seen since I left the Sonoran desert. The light pinks and purples and blues soon gave way to the most intense yellows, oranges and crimson. The sky was on fire and as such, I realized, my fire had been built for me.

The evening gently ushered in an amazing canopy of stars, planets and the moon. Everything from the daytime settled down as the crickets began their night song. Night hawks sang a strange noise overhead as they hunted small flying insects alongside the bats. Nocturnal animals began to go about their business, aware of my presence yet unperturbed. My eyes gradually adjusted to the darkness, and I discovered that I could see in the dark after all. Old perceptions continued to fall away as I began to deepen my experience through the continued fluidity of my assemblage point.

As the evening deepened I touched upon the abstract visions that I had earlier and recognized that my own internal rhythm began to match the rhythm of the natural world. Sharing one heart-beat, one pulse, helped me to remember that I am truly a piece of the whole in a very alive and vibrant universe.

As I lay there looking up at the night sky watching shooting stars, I began to cry tears of joy for the immense beauty all around me, in me. In aligning with silent knowledge, I recognized my connection to all things. A knowing arose. There is an exquisite balance to everything that goes back to the point of origin. Since the beginning of time, a most beautiful, unique, and diverse lineage has been emerging.

What became clear to me is that when we take the time to sit within nature, we gather power: just by sitting within it. We take in the beauty all around us and in so doing, we become beauty. As we begin to merge with our surroundings, we have no choice but to move in the flow of power, the power that flows throughout the universe. Language ceases, and as it does, reason ceases, opening us up to perceive in magical ways.

At some point during the evening I drifted off to sleep and into dream. Nayeli emerged from the dark sky with the millions of stars glittering behind her. I was elated to be in her presence and honored that she took the time and energy to join me here.

She smiled as she approached me saying, "As a female

warrior you have learned on your first day of la búsqueda to recognize that you already have everything you need. Sit on the Earth and honor her. Honor the sky, honor all the beings of the Earth, and you will be filled with silent knowledge. As each one of us increases our connection with the Earth and feel her pulse, we will be living the synergistic, co-creative life we were meant to be living. We will be completely aligned with the Earth's heartbeat and with Source. This is the most important part of our evolution as warriors and will lead you to total freedom. Sleep well, Nubecita."

Into the Heart of Darkness

> When you are centered and in balance with the earth,
> you are capable of amazing achievements. You can
> perceive the harmonic frequencies of the universe, even
> when surrounded by great turmoil, confusion, and
> strife, because you are immovable. You hold silence and
> true knowing in your heart.
> - Nayeli

The loud caw of a raven awakened me. With the sun just beginning to rise, I looked for the source of the noise to find the raven perched on a branch high in the tree next to me. Ravens have always fascinated me, and I often communicate with them in a back-and-forth dialogue by mimicking their sounds. They are known to have as many as thirty-five different vocalizations within their complex communication. I cawed at the raven in response. It cawed loudly, three more times, and then took flight.

My stomach reminded me that I had not had anything to eat for over twenty-four hours, but I didn't feel hunger. I took a small sip of water and went to relieve myself in the spot I selected for just this purpose.

I wrapped my blanket around me to keep out the morning chill and noticed the sky was cloudy and gray. I picked up my tarp and water bottles and decided to seek out a new space to spend the day, nearby, but different, thus finding a way to further shift my assemblage point and break away from familiarity.

I spoke my gratitude out loud to the spot that had been my home for the previous day and night and for the insights that I gleaned while there.

Walking only about five hundred yards, I came upon a very large and unique rock outcropping. I walked around to discover that it was styled like a natural amphitheater complete with a large and protective overhang. The mouth of the amphitheater faced the east. With its deep red sandstone and unusual contours, I felt very protected from the elements in the event that the weather took a turn for the worse.

I walked to the overhang and saw a bunch of sunflower seed shells, evidence of hikers. I hoped that none would come through as I put down my blanket, tarp, and water bottles, thereby staking my claim to this area.

I heard a distant rumble of thunder, but it was bright out in spite of the grayness, and there didn't appear to be any rainclouds. But a rainstorm can come in fast in the desert. Considering how cold it would be if it a storm did come in, I set about collecting dried juniper wood and tinder for a fire. I wanted to be prepared in case a storm did hit so I could stay reasonably warm during the night.

When I finished my lengthy yet rewarding task, I sat down on the soft red sand, facing the center of the amphitheater. I stared directly into the overhang and started to think about the ancient line and other information I received the night before. The colors of the rocks and boulders were deep red and yellow, constantly changing as the clouds shifted and the light changed. It was a beautiful setting, one that I came to appreciate fully in its pureness and wildness.

I sat up fully alert with that feeling you get when someone is staring at you. I turned around to find a coyote approaching me. I clapped my hands and yelled, "Go." It held its ground and stared at me. In that moment I came to the realization that this wasn't a coyote. It was larger and had a fuller face. Its eyes were piercing as it stared directly into mine, it had a lush coat and a big, bushy tail. The coyotes that I had encountered during my hikes were scraggly, and their tails would droop down between their rear legs. When you frightened a coyote, it would typically put its head down and scamper away. This was, by my calculation, a wolf.

The wolf assessed me, and I told myself to connect with the energy of the Earth and align with Source as I had done when the fawn had approached me. The sensations arising within me were of fear, however. I seemed certain that the joyful bond I had created with the fawn was not going to occur now. Something caught my eye and another wolf was slowly approaching. It's true that your life starts to pass before your eyes in moments of extreme fear. I could only think that El Cuervo would come looking for me when I didn't return, only to find my body parts and bones littering the amphitheater.

I jumped to my feet, clapped my hands, and said loudly, "Get out of here!" They watched me for about five seconds, which felt like an eternity, and proudly sauntered off, as if knowing that they had provoked and frightened me successfully.

I became agitated and edgy, trying so hard to rationalize why wolves would be in this area. The Mexican Gray Wolf which was being reintroduced to these areas was a possibility. Maybe they were coyotes, I told myself, but I have seen plenty of coyotes to know that they weren't, and besides, unlike coyotes, these two weren't afraid. I feared that they would return and pondered gathering my things and leaving, but I considered that these beautiful and stately creatures would present me with knowledge or awareness, even though they frightened me.

I convinced myself that the wolves were off chasing rabbits, when I heard the faintest sound coming towards the mouth of the amphitheater in which I now sat. And there it was, the wolf walking slowly towards me. Off to the right of it was the other one, and they were closing in. The small amphitheater didn't seem so protective anymore, and I began to feel an impending sense of doom. I quickly reached around the area in which I sat and grabbed rocks to pile up beside me as my only defense. They stopped and watched.

And then I saw two more coming in from a ridge on the left of the outcropping. Really? This was how I would die? Eaten for breakfast by a pack of wolves? I tried to convince myself that they weren't there, that some strange hallucination was occurring due to a lack of food, but I knew better.

The two on the ridge sat on their haunches watching as the two on the ground moved towards me again. They looked curious rather than threatening. When they moved to within twenty feet of me, my adrenaline started pumping and I began to throw the rocks at the ground in front of them screaming, "Go away! I don't have anything for you." They seemed to consider my command for they nobly turned, headed towards the two on the ridge, and then all four walked away.

I was torn: should I leave in the event they are working out a strategy to take me down or should I receive this event as a gift and sit with it and rest for the day and night? My mind raced. I felt vulnerable now and wasn't sure which direction to take.

Off in the far distance I heard a slow, steady drumbeat and knew that El Cuervo, who had intuitively picked up on my angst, had started to drum. I closed my eyes, inhaled a few deep breaths, and allowed myself to become centered between Earth and sky.

Just then Nayeli, whose voice seems to ride the wind, entered my field of consciousness and said, "Do not fear the wolves. They emanate a strong sense of family and have come out of curiosity and now include you as one of their own. Pay attention to the omens. They are bringing you a message."

"What kind of message, Nayeli?" I asked feebly.

"I do not know the answer to that. You must sit in silence and consider what that may be. The wolves would not have appeared unless you had requested to know something specific." And she was gone.

I sat very still for a long time on that red sand, the steady drumbeat connecting me to the pulse of the Earth. It started to rain lightly and the skies darkened. I heard the low rumble of thunder in the distance and felt the telltale sign of a storm approaching. I moved to the overhang just as a brilliant streak of lightning appeared followed shortly by a low rumble of thunder. The storm was getting closer.

I thought about the wolves that had approached me earlier, and based on what Nayeli told me and the insights about the ancient line that I received the previous day, I got the strong sense that they were attempting to show me the root of their own particular lineage. They were, after all, the original dog as it existed before man intervened.

A very dreamlike quality washed over me, and in it I found

myself leaning against a tree trunk in an aspen grove. It was as
though I had somehow transcended time and space and had
moved from this red desert country and into a subalpine forest.

I heard the howl of the wolves nearby but was no longer
alarmed. I thought again about what Nayeli had said, that they
are here to convey some kind of message. Prior to my quest I
asked El Cuervo what to do if mountain lions or bears had
approached me, even though it was unlikely. He assured me
that the animal's and my connection with the Source would
keep me protected, and that I had nothing to fear. I hadn't
asked about wolves, which were the furthest thing from my
mind.

The lightning streaked again and a loud clap of thunder
immediately followed. The storm was close. The alpha female
howled and the other three howled with her. It was as though
they were communicating a common message together. When
they were done with their beautiful song, I realized their
howling had put me into a trance, and I felt as though I had
passed through a new gateway and into yet another realm of
existence.

I began to receive, in a surreal, dreamlike quality, a series
of images. I saw a time when humans and animals once walked
freely across all terrains without any thoughts of becoming
enmeshed in patterns. Never following a pre-determined trail
and choosing to wander the paths less traveled, they ventured
out into the unknown with fearlessness and self-reliance. Most
of the animals and humans were engaging in a form of
cooperative hunting, a way to ensure their mutual survival.

I saw that some humans lived in caves, some out in the
open in temporary shelters. Besides hunting game, they

gathered edible plants and were adept in all stages of creation. Some tanned hides and made clothing or decorative adornments; others made tools, and still others wove baskets and created containers from various natural materials. They were in harmony with the Earth and with each other and had the foresight to know when they had made an impact on their environment. At these times they would pack up and venture out to find a new area in which to harvest their food and supplies so the area that they had depleted could reinvigorate itself.

I enjoyed these images immensely and felt, within myself, my own deep connection with the Earth and the other creatures that cohabitate upon her.

After a while I saw that groups of people were beginning to separate themselves from the natural flow of hunting and gathering. They had constructed stone dwellings and enclosure like areas in which to remain on a permanent basis. As I gained more clarity into what I saw, the enclosures revealed themselves to be pens that contained plants and animals. Scouts were dispatched to the forests for the purpose of gathering plants by the roots. The animals that they could catch would be brought back to the pens.

I saw some men and women pleading to return to the forests, some of them fleeing with their children, only to be captured and put to work managing crops and cleaning the animal pens.

It shocked me to perceive that people's connection to the Earth and to Spirit was being severed. Their powers of creation had been thwarted and in some cases, completely stripped from them. They were brainwashed into believing that their creations were inferior and became filled with feelings of unworthiness, and even shame. They eventually stopped trying to escape and retreated into their minds, no longer capable of functioning from their hearts.

I looked up sadly towards the ridge where I last heard the howl of the wolves. A ceaseless flow of images suddenly bombarded me, spinning all around me in a vast cyclone of energetic lines, all having to do with the destruction of the Earth and the species upon her. Water diversion and damming, mining, oil drilling, salinization, deforestation, overfishing, crowded and filthy factory farm animal feedlots, pollution, soil erosion, agribusiness, weather control, pharmaceuticals, declining health, human trafficking, child labor, human and animal cruelty, polluted water, wild animal poaching, extinction, corrupt governments, war.

I couldn't believe what I witnessed; I became so saddened and sickened at the atrocity of it all. I began to cry, horrified by the bombardment of the nightmarish vision I received. Repulsed and stricken to the core, my body reacted to this horrible reality by convulsing with dry heaves. To coerce people into separation from the natural world by telling them a better way existed was bad enough, but to attempt to dominate and control the natural environment and everything within it for profit and power was self-important, manipulative, and evil.

I tried to wrap my mind around what this vision was, though I already had a good idea. Suddenly the energies of greed, fear, hate, and control swirled around me like a cold, dark force. It gave me goose bumps and made the hair on the back of my neck stand up. I heard a whimpering coming from the direction of the ridge where the wolves sat quietly.

A shadow seemed to loom above me, darkening the already gray sky and I began to see and sense the traits of overconsumption, irresponsibility, and great disrespect creeping over the planet. I began to recognize that this pervasive energy sits in wait to consume everything upon the Earth in its entirety, including the land itself.

Just then a huge bolt of lightning struck. Simultaneously, an enormous and loud crack of thunder shook me deeply. As I looked towards the ridge the lightning illuminated the image of four wolves running off into the rain.

Pouring rain, thunder, and lightning raged. Gratitude filled me for the depth of the small overhang under which I sat and for the blanket I had brought with me. I also felt immense gratitude to have had the foresight for collecting fuel for a fire. There I sat, with my fire aglow and my blanket around my shoulders, staring out into the storm, and reeling in terror from all I had experienced.

Everything about what I had witnessed seemed so surreal to me. My mind was spinning as I tried to make sense of everything that had unfolded. My sense of time and space became jumbled. It seemed like the visions had lasted about an hour, yet I knew what I gained was more like an eight hour download of information. Beyond the man-made story that I perceived were the lines of energy that were simultaneously presenting themselves to me in connection to the atrocities occurring throughout the world. Exhausted, I threw some more wood on my fire.

I must have drifted off, although I still heard the roar of the storm in my dreamlike state. My mind, even in sleep, tried to make sense of everything I perceived throughout the onslaught of information. Where did what I called this dark force come from? What made it do the things it did? How is it able to succeed in creating such an illusory world to which the majority of humanity has become attached?

I suddenly awoke, agitated and aware. During another lightning strike I thought I saw a dark shadow at the edge of the amphitheater and then I heard the most inhuman scream arise from it. Terror gripped me once again, and I screamed as loud as I could: "Go away! You have no power here!" I raised my fist at the thundering sky and screamed, "Who is the keeper of the key?" It seemed as though the entire Earthly reality had become more like a computer program or an unnatural video game of barbaric proportion. Are we stuck in a program while some unearthly master looks down upon us maneuvering us around the playing field with a game controller?

While the storm continued in its fury, my dreams had been more like a bombardment of messages. Visions with little epiphanies emerged to help me to understand on a deeper level the dark force that lies across humanity's shoulders disguised as a soft and comfortable blanket. It felt to me like an endless wave of illusory concepts designed to sedate the masses, to keep them under the spell of control and confusion as it attempts to consume the life-force of everything in its path.

The visions continued and consisted of a man running in a hamster wheel, around and around, while he fed on dollars that anesthetized him, bloating him with a false sense of success, opportunity, and stability; his greatest fear: failure. A woman, conforming to the expectations placed upon her to be a productive member of the workforce, a devoted mother, a dutiful wife, while simultaneously ensuring that she maintain an unnaturally thin and youthful appearance while slowly dying inside, ignoring her own natural drive to connect with nature. Children, medicated on Ritalin, staring blankly at teachers who attempt to mold them into skilled individuals so they can support the economic wheels of consumption. Elderly people sent to nursing homes to die alone and terrified. So many people overindulging through food, alcohol, drugs, trying desperately to fill the void that exists from their lack of connection to the Earth.

I saw massive quantities of cows in stockyards being sent to painful and inhumane slaughter while others stood helpless, hooked up to hideous machines sucking life sustaining milk from their udders. Chickens standing on top of each other inside warehouses, never having seen the light of day being brutally killed. Pigs with numbers spray painted on their backs, trapped in stifling metal pens so small they couldn't even move. Worse still, sows were immediately separated from their piglets. I saw seas being overfished as countless forms of sea life were destroyed and discarded in a wake of imminent destruction.

My head ached and I cried out loud: "Make it stop, make it stop!" Oh how I wished El Cuervo was with me.

I could see it clearly now: the birth of the dark force all those years ago under the guise of civilization. A deceptive origin masked in the promise of salvation, a salvation that no one asked for and that no one needed. My blood pumped as the multitude of energetic lines became clear to me. I gained extreme insight as to what Nayeli had meant when she said that I have to recapitulate the lines of the world. We have allowed the position of our assemblage points to remain fixated upon that story. The man-made Story of Civilization.

The storm continued to rage its deluge of rain, thunder, and lightning. I placed more wood on the fire, wrapped myself in my blanket and tarp, and cried until, at last, I drifted into a deep and dreamless sleep.

Inner Silence

As warriors we must recognize that we already have everything we need. Sit on the earth and honor her, honor the sky, and you will be filled with silent knowledge. As each one of us increases our connection with the earth, we will be living as we were meant to be living; in reciprocity and balance.

- Alejandro

The sun beamed down on me, and I didn't know where I was at first. Disoriented, I opened my eyes and looked out of the mouth of the amphitheater, the sun rising and illuminating the entire expanse. Mist rose from the saturated ground. I breathed deeply and was greeted with the fresh, aromatic desert smell that is so invigorating and welcoming after a rainstorm.

The desert is an amazing place, and in spite of the torrents of rain the night before, the flowers of the Datura plant, a nocturnal bloomer also known as angel's trumpets, were just beginning to wither as the sun grew brighter. Hummingbird moths were flitting from flower to flower, drinking up the nectar of these beautiful and sweetly fragrant plants.

Lying peacefully, the events of the previous night threatened to infiltrate my mind, and I felt neither ready nor willing to revisit them. I sat up, took a swig of water and heard a loud whirring noise right by my head. Chirping shrilly, a hummingbird fluttered by to drink from a Datura flower. Then she buzzed herself to the top of the plant and sat, facing my direction. I have always loved hummingbirds and knew them to represent beauty, joy, and vibration. It is said that their wings beat in perfect harmony with their tiny, yet powerful hearts, which is quite amazing when you consider that their wings beat around seventy times per second.

She was a beautiful, ruby-throated hummingbird with mostly green and white feathers. Her sharp little eyes were looking at me and she turned her head from side to side, looking at me through each eye. She took flight, chirping and whirring high into the sky and then zoomed back down right in front of me. She was hovering, and I could hear her wings buzzing through their rapid vibration. After a few seconds she returned to her perch on the Datura plant.

After what had occurred yesterday I mindfully considered what the omen of a hummingbird might represent. The hummingbird's vibrations had me thinking about my task of energetically connecting to all of the lines of awareness. I remembered when Nayeli had explained to me about the pulse of the Earth; she had said this pulse surrounds and protects all living things with a natural frequency vibration.

I closed my eyes and offered up my gratitude for weathering the storm that had passed as well as the awareness of the dark force that had arisen. I thanked the wolves for their presence and for the sunshine and warmth of this new day. I thanked the hummingbird for her beautiful energy and vibration.

I finally eased myself up from my resting place and stretched. As I did so, three hummingbirds buzzed in, chasing each other and twittering noisily. I took this as a good sign, folded my tarp and blanket, picked up my water bottles, and thanked the spot for keeping me safe. It was time to find another spot in which to spend this new and glorious day, and I eagerly moved on.

I exited through the mouth of the amphitheater and wandered towards the east, the place of the rising sun. After walking for about half an hour, the topography of the land changed significantly, and I found myself in a very flat and open area speckled with juniper trees and huge rock formations that looked like ancient sentinels. I followed what appeared to be a dry wash to a magnificent old juniper, her huge trunk cracked and weathered, her limbs twisted and gnarled. I immediately loved her and knew that this would be my spot for this third and final day and night of la búsqueda.

I spread my tarp on the ground, laid my blanket upon it, and sat with my side against the trunk of the big juniper. I pressed my ear against her rugged bark and listened. And soon she spoke. She told me that we have to become conduits like trees so we can bridge the energy of the earth as it moves up through our bodies and into the warmth and light of the sun. This allows us to merge with the realm of the infinite.

I entered into a state of heightened awareness, and I observed how some luminous fibers were connected from tree to tree. Some were free floating in the subtle breeze, unanchored, some were connected to the earth. And then I felt surrounded by affection, a deep, penetrating affection. I knew beyond the shadow of a doubt that this affection was emanating from all the trees surrounding me. They were watching me, feeling my energetic frequency, my connection to them, to the earth, the sun, the cosmos.

I moved effortlessly into a state of absolute silence, listening to the birds and the other noises of this beautiful morning. Suddenly, I heard the familiar whirring of the hummingbird and looked up to see this tiny little bird perched on a branch above me. I perceived the bird as verification that my spot was perfect.

As I sat in silence, I merged with the pulse of the Earth. I realized that she facilitated the awakening of my vibrational frequency, bringing me to states of higher consciousness and into realms of deeper awareness. I felt light and empty and was cognizant of the fact that when we allow ourselves to sit in silence, we provide ourselves with the opportunity to become empty vessels through which Source energy may flow. With my mind free of my previously held thoughts, I had become empty. I reunited my connecting link with universal life-force energy.

Nayeli, dancer on the wind, appeared in my thoughts and honored me for making it through such a challenging night, and for paying attention to the omens. She implied that as beings of pure energy, when we live our lives with an attitude of gratitude for all that the Earth provides for us, we become aligned with the energy of all of creation. In this alignment we are able to witness the oneness of creation as it unfolds. And when we witness the magical beauty of creation we are able to align with the silent flow of primal energy, thus leading to our own creative evolution while duality dissolves.

I breathed in the Earth deeply, drawing the breath through my nostrils as well as energetically up from the Earth directly into my root chakra. I began to feel very energetically balanced between Earth and sky, and with the external vibrational frequency that surrounded me. I felt buoyant and whole. My scope of perception became heightened, and I experienced a great shift in awareness. My heart chakra felt as though it were ready to burst, and I felt overcome by an immense feeling of awe and admiration for the opportunity to be alive.

Something caught my attention, and I looked towards a rock that was about one foot high to see, just above it, the tiny head of a snake peering at me. It was so cute, and must have been extended the length of its entire body, balancing on its tail to watch me. I laughed gleefully at the beauty of the moment and watched it as it slowly descended and slithered away.

I realized that I had nothing to do and nowhere to go, to just remember myself. As I did I began to see the beauty of the universe emerging within my mind's eye. With utter clarity I could feel my body resonating, emanating my ability to remain in a state of stillness and presence as the world continued to move without me. A bridge was created and a new band of awareness was being assembled.

It felt as though I observed myself from space, looking down at a tiny dot, which was me, on a gorgeous blue planet. I remembered having resided out there in the cosmos, as pure conscious awareness, with the power to manifest myself into form upon this planet. So I did.

An avalanche of awareness began to tumble into me. These were things I felt certain that I knew without having any idea that I knew them. A knowing arose that we are pure awareness or pure consciousness within our form and for many reasons we have become limited from our potential to expand beyond the boundaries of our physical containers. As we move into deeper levels of awareness, through our connection with the Earth and our commitment to silence, we are able to increase our energetic life-force essence and reconnect with the energetic vibrational frequencies of the universe.

The whirring of the hummingbird brought me back from my reverie. I watched as she flitted among the brilliant red Indian paintbrush flowers. I thanked her for bringing her vibrations to help me remember and moved from the base of the juniper tree and into the sun. Then I thanked the old, grandmother tree.

I stood with my arms outstretched facing the sun feeling more alive and balanced than I had in a long time. The events of the past two days and nights seemed ages ago and I only had now, this moment, to appreciate and experience. Wandering around the area, I reflected on what I had just perceived and why Nayeli was so adamant about me undertaking this amazing and powerful task of connecting with the pulse of the Earth to enter into silent knowledge.

Like an explosion in the center of my being, a feeling of deep awe, respect, wonder, and admiration opened up. There is a divine and sacred connecting link to Source. I became aware that my mind had been clouded with the compulsory illusions of what it means to exist as a human being based on upholding patterns that had been imposed upon mankind for centuries. To be able to sit within my own experience, without distractions, provided me with the insight into that which is possible. I came to understand what it means to be a part of the world in my own creative way.

Watching lizards darting here and there and bees buzzing from flower to flower, and ants working unwaveringly to contribute to their community, I felt humbled and stunned to see the world in this new way. My enhanced level of perception assisted me in moving beyond the paradigms of life and living as I had been told. My energetic level felt inexhaustible as though I sat at the center of creation with unlimited potential. I longed to once again create and co-create with the energy of the universe in a dance of harmonic frequencies and vibrations, the ones that I sensed were the very frequencies through which we arrived on this planet in the first place.

Feeling fluid and free, I danced, unencumbered under the heat of the sun in this extraordinary and gorgeous desert. Touching the Earth with my finger tips and raising my arms to the sky, I spun and twirled rolling my head around and around. I felt that the world was at my fingertips and all I had to do was point to a spot on the ground in order to create a flower. Or wave my hand through the air with a series of fluttery motions to produce a bird. Every cell in my body was vibrating and I felt cleansed, pure, energized, and in complete balance with everything.

I became the essence of all things simultaneously. The essence of the Earth, the essence of sound, the essence of the plants, the rocks, and of all the creatures in the co-creative act of manifesting whatever my heart desired. I now knew that I am a multi-dimensional being, ancient and infinite, experiencing the wonder and awesomeness of this beautiful planet. I lay on the Earth and a deep, steady sound simultaneously emitted from it and from myself. It felt so primordial, so ancient, it seemed that the totality of the universe was woven into that very sound. I lay there for a long time taking in the sounds and the silence of the desert before drifting off to sleep.

It was the middle of the night when I awoke. An amazing canopy of stars blanketed me. With no moon, the stars sparkled brilliantly. I found my way to the juniper tree and wrapped my blanket around me. Moving away from the tree I lay down on the ground to take in the magnificent star field above me.

Off in the distance I heard some coyotes playfully yipping. The incredible sense of oneness that I felt with all things overwhelmed me. I thought about how our connection with the Earth allows us to align ourselves with primal energy. This brings us to a state of universal oneness, and we become free of the patterns of humanity. Our innate ability to truly live as the self-empowered and creative beings that we are is restored.

Further musings brought me to the discovery that when we allow ourselves to sit in the wilderness and become still, we are able to gather the necessary energy to know ourselves more fully, specifically as a creative force within an extensive energy field of creative forces. This knowledge brought me a sense of great joy and I felt an inward release of abundant energy within my body. The energies of the stories and patterns that had been imposed upon me and had taken over my mind, my very soul, had finally dissolved, and I found myself completely aligned with the power of creation.

I recognized that to be in the natural flow of life, everything becomes effortless. There is a strong sense and knowing that everything is sacred. With a new and hopefully lasting ability to view situations from all possible perspectives, I felt relieved to discover that the entire unfolding of reality around us is pure and complete. When our life-force vibration is in equilibrium with all other forces, we become empowered to utilize our individual will combined with Source energy to create and co-create effectively.

Images filled my mind as I saw people reconnecting with the Earth in honor and respect, recognizing, once again, the importance of living in balance with her, giving gratitude to her for all of the resources that she so selflessly provides for our sustenance.

What unfolded before me was like a beautiful dream. Men, women, and children lay down the distractions of the world to sit in silence and listen to the voice of the planet.

A young man in his late twenties went backpacking through the rugged Canyonlands. He was equipped with a tent, sleeping bag, water, and minimal rations. He stumbled upon remote and ancient ruins that lay undisturbed. They were hidden by juniper trees at the mouth of a small cave that had been created from giant stones sheared off of a cliff thousands of years ago. Within the ruins he saw ancient pottery and stone tools. He set down his heavy pack and sat for a time in the coolness of the shelter, closing his eyes and breathing in what life might have been like in those times.

Beyond time and space he witnessed, with reverence, the synergy that the ancient ancestors had with their environment. They wanted nothing and were provided with all that they needed. Inhaling to the center of his being, he felt a stirring deep within himself that he too, had everything he needed. Filled with respect and awe of this ancestral connection to the Earth, he left the ruins knowing that his life was forever altered. He took nothing and left no trace he had been there.

Transported to a clearing in the canyon near a stream, a

young woman appeared in the periphery of my eyesight. I turned my head slightly to watch her as she disrobed and placed her hiking boots and clothing in a small stack upon a rock. She knelt on the soft sand and moved her lithe body into a yoga child pose, her arms outstretched before her as she embraced the Earth. She released into the Earth the stresses of her life, becoming an empty vessel.

A gentle breeze blew in from the north to wash over her. Paying attention to this omen of cleansing and renewal she rose to her feet, arms extended wide to the sky in gratitude for the very fact that she was part of the creation that surrounded her. She danced in rhythm to the sounds of the Earth, joyful and free and energized. Kneeling at the edge of the stream she washed herself; she was ready to face the world anew, bringing with her the peace and the unity she felt throughout her entire body, confirmation that she was one with all things.

Exuberant laughter arose and I turned, once again, to look towards the direction of its source. A handful of children were leaping from boulder to boulder that surrounded the campsite in which their families had settled for the weekend. Squeals of delight were released as the children, who felt like pioneers in the wilderness, found feathers and shiny stones and flowers and sticks in the shapes of animals throughout the underbrush.

Exploring a small cave filled them with wonder and fright as they went deeper into the gap. Screaming and squealing, the girls ran from the cave frightened by the sight of hundreds of daddy long legs while the boys, unperturbed, marveled at a pack rat nest they had found.

All of these people were giving themselves the time to decompress from the trials of daily life. Rested, relaxed, and invigorated from the energies of the Earth, they were able to return to their jobs, daily tasks, and school, each filled with their own stories of adventure and connection in a heightened state of awareness.

As a result of restoring this connection with Earth and Spirit, I observed as healthy and content communities of people lived in a state of abundance. Grateful for what they had, they no longer lived within the illusion of not having enough and the accompanying need to consume more.

I watched as programs were introduced into schools at the elementary level teaching children about the power of the Earth. Information about wholesome foods, animal welfare, and hands-on gardening taught them how to honor and respect the Earth, and thus, themselves and one another. An entire fifty minute school period, once a week, was dedicated to sitting outdoors in silence. Music and dancing was incorporated into their curriculum. As a result of these programs, the imaginations of children expanded, bringing them to states of peace and well-being, providing them with awareness and knowledge about life that can only be experienced.

I saw entire workforces of people from all walks of life succeed in renewable resource companies implementing wind and solar power, biomass, geothermal and hydroelectric energies. The era of fossil fuel energies and drilling platforms were now historical, which ensured clean air, a stable climate, and environmental balance.

I saw people driving electric cars powered by the sun and commuting on magnetic levitation trains, a free, unlimited, clean and green energy supply. The air was no longer polluted.

People lived in smaller houses and were happier with less.

Crime and violence reached an all-time low and prisons were closing down.

Wild animals and sea mammals populated the planet in rich abundance. Wildlife poaching, once considered a misdemeanor act in many areas, now carried strict and costly penalties and nearly ceased altogether. Over-harvesting of the oceans was reduced by closing off certain seas to fishing for several years at a time, allowing for the fish populations to reach a healthy balance once again.

People were evolving, becoming aware, responsible and self-sustaining. Combined energies and harmonic acts of creation were in progress all over the world. No longer driven by greed and power, the inhabitants of the Earth worked for the good of the whole. Food was free of harmful pesticides and GMO's, livestock was raised on farms, not in overcrowded, disease prone feedlots, and the beef industry declined significantly reducing the need for deforestation. In addition, the amount of CO_2 from methane gas into the atmosphere decreased considerably as had water consumption by feedlots. People had an abundant, clean water supply.

It seemed that the whole of creation was content. People transformed their work from assignments to fulfill for those in power to their creative playground. They were healthier, happier, safer, friendlier, and more harmonious with their natural surroundings and each other.

Somewhere off in the distance I heard what sounded like multiple drums beating as one. I considered that it was El Cuervo and the multiple drums were the result of an echo off of the canyon walls. The drumbeat merged with the heartbeat of the earth. I began to lose myself to the combined beats as they harmonized in rhythmic unison. It seemed to me that life was far simpler than we had ever thought. All we have to do is align with the forces of nature, with honor and respect.

I pulled the blanket around me, ready to depart to the dream world, wondering how my dreams might change as a result of feeling so new in the world. I felt so peaceful and content, as though I could stay out here in this desert forever. But I also anticipated with excitement the return to the comforts of my world.

Integration

Within the silence, existing awareness is deepened, and new awareness is encountered. Pure knowing emerges, energy is amassed, and the integration of first and second attention knowledge occurs. As a result, the assemblage point shifts, and one is provided the opportunity to move forward from a new reference point, while perceiving everything from within a new band of awareness of their own creation.
- El Cuervo

On this, the final morning since I had set out to accomplish my task, I awoke to a cacophony of birdcalls, warm sunshine, and morning dew. With my senses revitalized, I saw with microscopic vision. I heard with ultrasonic ears, and I smelled everything in a complete and new way. I sensed the heartbeat of the Earth and knew that her pulse moved through me, through all of us, at all times. With humble gratitude and reverence, I thanked the juniper tree, the hummingbirds, the stars, and the Earth. I picked up my tarp, blanket, and water bottles, and started my walk back to the camp.

The impact the past few days had on me would take some time to completely solidify. I had a lot of information to absorb and was looking forward to returning to Sonora to discuss everything with El Cuervo, Nayeli, and Alejandro.

As I walked towards our campsite I saw El Cuervo by the

camp stove pouring a cup of coffee. He looked up at me and said smiling, "Welcome back, Nubecita. How did it go?"

After he hugged me, I sat down at the picnic table, and he brought me some cool water and fresh fruit then joined me with his cup of coffee. We sat in silence for a long time while I ate a few grapes, a banana and pieces of an apple. I looked at him as though I'd never seen him before. He looked different or perhaps, I perceived him differently.

"I am so hungry!" I exclaimed.

He laughed and said he knew the feeling. El Cuervo had engaged in various forms of la búsqueda; questing, camping alone, retreating into the wilderness, and was very familiar with spending much time alone in nature.

"Well then, let's get this train rolling and go get a proper breakfast," he said.

We set about packing up the pick-up, again mostly in silence. I wanted to communicate with El Cuervo, so much was spinning in my head, and yet I couldn't find any words. After a final check of our area, making sure that we left no trace, no sign that we had even been to this spot, we got into the pick-up and headed towards the main road.

"I'd like to head back towards Sonora if that's okay with you, El Cuervo. There is so much that I want to discuss with Nayeli, Alejandro, and you. We can talk about some of it on the way; I can't believe how much has happened in such a short period of time. So much is revealed when we enter into silence!" I exclaimed.

"It sure is," he said. "When we take time to truly listen to the messages from the earth, from the Universe, we are able to refine and sharpen our seeing. Yes, let's go, I'm ready to head back too. It'll be a long drive and will give you a chance to decompress."

We drove for about an hour, mostly in silence, until we came to a town that had a roadside restaurant. We went in, and I ate an enormous breakfast of oatmeal, fresh strawberries and blueberries, eggs over easy, wheat toast, and fresh brewed coffee. It was the best meal I could remember eating in a long time, especially since I had not eaten for days. El Cuervo laughed at the fact that I ate everything on my plate and asked me if I wanted to order dessert. We laughed, paid the bill and hit the road.

We took Route 191 southbound and after driving for nearly nine hours we decided to regroup, eat, and camp in Silver City, New Mexico. We had driven mostly in silence as I processed the events of the past week, listened to some music, and slept sporadically. We were up before sunrise the next morning and drove to the Mexican border at Douglas, Arizona. Once through, we got onto Route 2 and headed towards Santa Ana, where we ate a late breakfast at one of our favorite restaurants, then headed towards Hermosillo. We would be at Nayeli's in a few hours, and I looked forward to seeing her again and to finally take a shower.

The intense and depthful feeling of presence and connection that I experienced during la búsqueda continued to pulsate throughout my body; it seemed as though I could even feel it moving through my hair.

Why is it so difficult, I pondered, for people to experience each new moment as it unfolds? How can we possibly evolve into deeper levels of awareness when we repeatedly permit deceptive patterns to remain in charge of our reality, dictating which patterns we should replicate to maintain the status quo? It is impossible to awaken into higher levels of consciousness if we continue living our lives in alignment with the stories that have been told to us. We must allow ourselves to feel, see, hear, and know our world from a place of stillness, a place of Spirit, and a place of pure perception.

"What'cha thinking about, Nubecita?"

I returned from my thoughts in the passenger seat of the pick-up and realized that I had been lost in dream for a very long time.

"So," I began excitedly trying to convey my thoughts to El Cuervo, "when we operate from a state of silence and presence, our identities emerge on the level of a creative Spirit. We come to recognize ourselves as beings who are free to choose and create from the infinite possibilities that are available to us. We learn to utilize free will to align with the harmonic frequencies that best suit our nature and assist us in living as a being in form. This is not because someone told us that this is the way we have to do it, but because we are openly intuiting the nature of our essence within the flow of universal life-force energy as our ultimate Source. When we are able to do this we are moving from a state of pure consciousness, no longer bound by the structure and form through which we were trained to identify."

"Well, that was a loaded statement," replied El Cuervo with his gentle and familiar laugh. I still felt the after effects of sitting for so long in silence. "What are you trying to tell me?" he asked.

"I now understand why it is so difficult to be able to trust in the flow of life because in order to do so, we must make a conscious choice to not allow our minds to control our every moment, our every thought. When we take a stand to be in our power, we come to recognize that our power isn't really ours, per se, but belongs to the flow of the universe that is guiding us, providing for us, and orchestrating our life's events with or without our approval or consent," I said.

The impact of what I said hit me. "Wow! That was by far the most powerful thing I have ever done. Just sitting for three days and nights, not doing anything. Simply and truly experiencing the world, the universe, in its purest form. Sorry, I don't mean to babble. So much revealed itself!"

"Babble on," El Cuervo encouraged, "I love listening to you and hearing your insights. I appreciate that you are comfortable sharing your dance with me. You were quiet for so long, I began to wonder if you had completely returned yet."

I smiled and reflected briefly on how much I respect and admire El Cuervo. He never got bored listening to me, even when I became repetitive or rambled on, which was my natural tendency when too excited, especially when I processed through something. He was equally as content to sit with me in silence.

Interrupting my thoughts about him he said, "So now that you've communed intensely with Source energy, it sounds as though you have a lot more knowledge."

"I now know that I know nothing," I laughed. In fact, saying that put me on the verge of hysterical laughter, and El Cuervo was driving, looking straight ahead with a huge smile on his face. "That knowledge or wisdom reveals itself," I continued, "when we are most open and ready to receive it. The wisdom, knowledge, or message that we receive is incorporated into our being and is therefore independent of a self-important reflection."

I felt strange saying this, as though I had to renounce what I considered to be my precious, hard-earned knowledge in the pursuit of deepening more fully into wisdom or true knowing. I realized that in order to accomplish this, I must be willing to have my own experiences on which to create my reality.

The only knowledge that we should hold is the knowledge that we must learn to look within ourselves. It is the center of consciousness within ourselves that allows us to remember our true origins. Like the peeling away of the layers of an onion, she who loses herself does indeed find herself at the very center.

"Do you know that I felt my heart open up to the universe, which led me to such a strong sense of awe and appreciation? I felt as though my entire being was simultaneously receiving and reflecting such an immense feeling of gratitude. I felt aligned with the entire universe and was able to feel that our connection with every living thing is an extension of the great energetic flow of awareness, serving as the most transformative and powerful force in the universe. The energy that flows through us is the universal life-force of pure primal energy that resides within us and simultaneously all around us. It is in everyone and everything that we hold awareness of."

El Cuervo pondered this for a while and said, "Our biggest challenges seem to occur when we decide to disassemble the façade that we've been hiding behind so we may embrace our authentic self. As pure Source energy begins to emerge from within us, a type of battle ensues as the false self that we've been masquerading as challenges us to uphold the safety net of familiarity. The lies that reside in our mind want desperately to maintain the patterns and stories that have served as the foundation of our existence. The mind and reason become threatened as universal life-force essence and Spiritual wholeness begin to envelop our human form. As human beings traveling towards balance and freedom, we are uniting with our own selves and in the process, with the entirety of creation. When this occurs, we have arrived at the gateway of the heart."

He told me how arriving at the gateway of the heart allows us to recognize, perhaps for the first time, our true nature. It is while we are in this heart space that we come to recognize the things that have served as distractions to our connection with the true nature of being. This true nature of being allows us to discover that we are much more than we have been told. There is nothing to do and nothing to learn, all we have to do is remember ourselves. When we remember ourselves, we are able to see the beauty of this universe with utter clarity. Our very soul becomes revealed and renewed, and we vibrationally emanate our ability to be in a state of stillness and presence as the world continues to move without us. Our vibrations, aligned with truth, have a way of touching others. If those people are open and paying attention, they will come to find themselves moving closer to the beautiful truth and stillness within themselves.

"In spite of your enthusiasm," he continued, "it is important at this point to fully integrate your state of being. Integration is essential and includes mindfulness. Once our hearts become open to the realm of Spirit, we must take action from within the space of Spirit. If we don't take the action necessary to integrate our newfound understanding and intuition into our lives, then all we really have done was experience a high moment that we can talk about, if we choose.

The real goal is to reunite with the Source energy of our existence."

"What do you mean by integration?" I asked.

"As we continue to increase consciousness, we begin to realize how each whole becomes part of a larger whole which is, itself, part of a larger whole. Through the integration of each of these realms of consciousness, we are able to, as part of the overall cosmic process, evolve and attain a holistic level of being. It becomes apparent that we, or at the very least, our minds and psyche, are aspects of the cosmos. Through our commitment and ultimate surrender towards growth, we have no choice but to develop and evolve naturally in the same manner as everything within the cosmos appears to do.

"By paying attention to the things that reveal themselves from silence, we are able to make the necessary adjustments to ease our transition into living our lives more fully aligned with the Earth and ultimately with Source," he said with finality.

We were quiet for a while, as I sat processing everything we had exchanged. My head felt so full and, in spite of my mounting excitement and curiosity, was beginning to ache dully.

"So," I asked, "in each and every moment, we are surrounded by eternity, and we are always connected within it and to it in all directions?"

"Yes. What you have experienced has shown you that beyond our state of existence in human form, we are pure awareness or pure consciousness within our form. For many reasons we have become restricted from our potential to expand beyond the boundaries of our physical vessels. As we move into deeper levels of awareness through our connection with the Earth and our commitment to silence, we are able to increase our energetic life-force essence and reconnect with the energetic vibrational frequencies of the universe. As we begin to integrate and move into new levels of awareness, we become capable of perceiving more deeply and begin to function at a higher energetic frequency.

"If we deny ourselves the opportunity to fully integrate our experiences, we stand to lose that knowledge or the specific insights that came to us when we return to our lives as we've known them to be."

"How will I integrate everything?" I asked.

"Mostly through conversation. Giving yourself the opportunity to talk with me, Nayeli, and Alejandro will allow you to express and remember what you experienced. You will begin to discover how these new insights help your world to become more inclusive to multiple dimensionalities of your being along with the wholeness that occurs when your mental, physical, and spiritual principles unite."

"The way I understand it," I said, hoping to solidify my understanding of our discussion, "is that as we evolve and experience unification, we recognize that we are but a small piece of a much larger whole. Through our commitment and ultimate surrender to awareness, we have no choice but to develop and evolve naturally in the same manner as everything within the cosmos does. Am I on the right track?"

"Yes, you are absolutely on the right track. As you continue to hone awareness you will undoubtedly come to find that we are part of an amazing and organized whole that pulses creatively throughout the entire cosmos. What can be more magical?" he concluded.

It seemed to me that our journey through eternity will be

an exciting venture, not in the actual knowing of what we will do, see, or explore but of the mystery that will unfold and reveal itself. I pondered what other possible acts of creation may exist beyond our current capacity to create.

It occurred to me that I am no longer afraid to die. There is nothing to be afraid of. I understand that we are a part of power, the same power that flows through the universe. Our life in form upon this planet is part of our cosmic journey of awareness and discovery. The fabric of our existence is part of the warp and weft of all existence. We are each a piece of an evolutionary cosmic weaving. Working together on this tapestry, we have the ability to transform the energetic fibers of disconnected, collective disorder into one of beauty and collaborative unity.

The Lineage

The Source of all things is in everything, everywhere, though many have forgotten. When we become free from the distractions of the world, planetary intelligence will awaken within us, and we can continue to evolve the natural and primal vision, the very creation that inspires the universe.
- Alejandro

"Lorraine" Nayeli called out from the kitchen, "don't forget to bring your tablet with you so you can show all of those beautiful pictures you took to Alejandro!"

Yes, I had taken pictures of everything, movies too. I loved my camera and my phone for such purposes and had synced everything to my tablet since arriving home. After a long, hot shower the night before and a hearty dinner that Nayeli prepared of shredded beef, fresh salsa, guacamole, and warm corn tortillas, El Cuervo and I showed Nayeli all the photos I had taken.

Other than telling her that everything on the trip and la búsqueda had been fantastic, we said little because we had plans to go to Alejandro's house to discuss everything together in detail. I met Nayeli and El Cuervo in the kitchen, and we packed all of the leftovers from the previous evening's dinner and headed out to the pick-up.

As we pulled down Alejandro's driveway, we could see him sitting under the huge cottonwoods. He waved to us, and while Nayeli and El Cuervo brought the food into the house, I ran to him and gave him a big hug.

"You look absolutely radiant, Nubecita," he said to me. "You are all afire with Spirit and are exuding an amazing glow."

"You are all aglow, too," I laughed and sat down on one of the Adirondack chairs next to him.

El Cuervo and Nayeli approached, and Alejandro stood again as they greeted him. Alejandro sat back down on what everyone knew to be his cottonwood stump; El Cuervo reclined in the hammock, and Nayeli sat in another Adirondack chair. I began to show Alejandro the photos of the red rock formations in Canyonlands, that I had taken when El Cuervo and I scouted the area, and told him that was where I chose to do la búsqueda.

"What a beautiful place to choose. These rock formations look like ancient ancestors, sentinels to eternity. The colors are amazing," he said while swiping through the pictures. "So, tell us about your journey."

"Okay," I said, "but I think I'm going to have a lot of questions for the two of you."

I told them about how I made a connection with and felt the pulse of the Earth and about all of the lines of energy I began to see. "I saw many, many lines of energy, glowing brightly."

"What were the lines that were glowing brightly, Nubecita?" asked Alejandro.

"I hoped you could tell me. There were so many of them. They were beautiful and so captivating. I felt compelled to merge with them and in some ways feel as though I already have. What are they?" I asked.

"Oh, they are a great many things," said Alejandro. "The brightest are the lines of happiness, beauty, sensuality, ambition, excitement, and love to name a few."

"No wonder they looked so beautiful," I exclaimed. "They powerfully drew me to them and made me feel so energized. Why do they appear as such bright lines and why were they there?"

"They are bundles of energetic lines, luminous fibers and emanations, swirling around the Earth, some of which have been flowing since the beginning of time. They are there to attract people to them," he said.

"Or distract them," said El Cuervo under his breath.

"What do you mean?" I asked.

Alejandro then surprised me by saying, "Some of the lines are of anger, fear, greed, despair, violence, and unworthiness, to name some of the brighter yet less virtuous lines."

"Well then why are they so beautiful?" I asked, anxious to understand.

"To distract people," El Cuervo said again.

"What do you mean to distract people?" I asked.

El Cuervo remained quiet, yielding to Alejandro's or Nayeli's knowledge on the subject.

"The lines, as you have witnessed, are bright and beautiful," Nayeli said. "The brightest lines are the lines into which people place a lot of energy. This makes them shiny and brilliant which appeals to the subconscious and attracts people to them easily, like moths to a flame. People provide a lot of energy to those lines by being exposed to the constant bombardment of subliminal messaging they receive through the stories, realities, beliefs, and judgments of others. These subliminal messages are fed to the public, and the public, without even realizing it, attaches a lot of importance to those lines. They become brighter as the result of collective consciousness feeding them. It's been going on for centuries. Many of those lines are man-made and have increased energetically through the world of reason. This has caused them to become anchored in reality."

"So the lines that are glowing brightly were doing so, not because of how good they are, but because of the amount of energy they are receiving from people?" I asked to bring clarity to my understanding. Without waiting for a response I said, "So that explains the big, dull line I saw. It wasn't dull and lusterless because it was a bad line but because nobody had energized it."

"Tell us about that line, Nubecita," said Alejandro leaning forward and resting his arms on his thighs.

Everyone was really quiet, and I sat thinking, reconnecting myself to that night in the desert, fibers of energy swirling all around me as I attempted to discover it again. I finally saw it.

"A line was laying before me that I found myself very attracted to. It was really dull and didn't seem to have a strong vibration like the other lines. It piqued my curiosity so I followed it for quite a ways. This line, as I came to perceive it, is the line that unites us with the Earth. For some reason, it fascinated me, and I began to wander further down the length of it."

I told them all that I could remember, about seeing what seemed like millions of years back to a time when fires were glowing brightly, and the line was vibrant with energy. I told them of how the feeling inside of me, while on that line, was one of peace, balance, and fluidity. It was as though that line gently supported me and urged me to move in accord with a flow that was far greater than I could comprehend or define. Then I asked, to no one in particular, what that specific line was.

All remained quiet. I looked at Nayeli, and it was obvious that she was waiting for Alejandro to respond, which he at last did. "You were walking along the line of the Lineage, the oldest line of awareness on Earth. In fact, it is as old as the Earth itself. It is the line of energy that connects all beings to Source, to the fire within the Earth. It is a lineage to which all humanity is a part and is not specific to any single path, tribe, culture, or philosophy.

"People of the Lineage are those who live in balance with the Earth, experiencing the wonder and awe of her power and her beauty. They walk gently upon her and through their alignment with Source, they are able to exist within the flow of infinity that permeates their very existence. They respect and honor the Earth and all her beings by connecting fully with her, in gratitude and with admiration. Because they have come to know her as a provider and nurturer, they are able to provide for and nurture others in the simplest and most natural ways without impacting her greatly.

"We live in an endless universe of energy, of forms, and yet as a culture we are forgetting that we have a very deep connection with nature, the very thing we must depend upon for our existence here on Earth. When we are connected through our awareness of the Earth, we are able to exist in balance. This balance comes about by completely connecting with the energy of the Earth. In this way, as you have done on la búsqueda, you became completely aligned with the emanations of the Earth. As a result you are balanced within the point of origin and connected with the Lineage. This is what brings you into full alignment with Source.

"If one is not connected with the Earth, they will find it difficult to align with Source. They may think they are aligned with Source when in fact, they have become aligned with the other emanations, the bright, luminous lines that we have just talked about. Those lines, as Nayeli explained, are not always the best. Their radiance is the result of the enormous amount of energy given to them. More often than not they are man-made fibers that are far removed from the Lineage, unbalanced and disconnected."

I expressed to them the deep sadness that I felt in seeing how dim the fires were along that line, and Nayeli said, "The Lineage is fading away because the flames of awareness are dying. Those flames of awareness, that live within every single being, are what feed this particular line. As more and more fires dwindle within the beings of the Earth, the fire that fuels the Earth itself will die. When this happens, the Earth will become a frozen, dead planet within the solar system."

"Why are the flames of awareness dwindling?" I asked.

"The Lineage," Alejandro began, "is the ancient energy of what it means to be human and it is diminishing at a rapid rate. That's why you saw the flames of awareness dying. The Lineage has been upheld for eons by people who are true seers and can perceive the Lineage for what it is. They have been known as Mystics, Sages, Shaman, Prophets, Spiritualists, Medicine People, Wisdom Keepers, and Elders. These people have been working diligently for many centuries to help a very confused species to remember. Unfortunately, there are so many distractions and diversions that tie humans to the illusions of materiality. This separates them from the pure essence of energetic awareness from which they originated."

I digested what he was telling me and asked him if Buddha and Jesus were Mystics.

"Oh yes, indeed they were. Extraordinary seers, in fact, who were able to effortlessly shift the fixation of the assemblage point of masses of people, with few words, to bring them closer to the truth. You can say that they were attempting to close the gap that had been created which caused the illusion of separation from Source and every other living thing. They were trying to rekindle the fires of awareness," he said.

"They were so successful," he continued, "that over time they became their own religious icons. Sadly, however, their visions and messages became diluted and weakened. Over time, they lost their original profundity and strength. Spiritual beliefs, much like everything else in the world, have experienced religious globalization. This became glaringly apparent during the last century when people took components from a wide range of Spiritual beliefs that they liked, threw away the parts they didn't like, and then followed a conglomeration of beliefs based on what was comfortable to them and easy to understand. In this century's long process of watering down and weakening ancient understanding, complex and profound nuggets of truth have vanished.

"The internet has further compounded the seriousness of the dilution of truths. People have become skimmers, meaning that if they want to come to understand something, they just skim through the contents of several websites. Rather than going out on the land to have an experience, they google what they want to know. After deriving the information that they find to be agreeable to them, they believe themselves to be authorities on the subject without having any wisdom about it. The danger in this is that they are taking the word of others as truth rather than investing any personal time into discovering what something really means. There is just no substitute for personal experience."

"Then how did the mystics and other seers convey their knowledge about the Lineage to people? Did they tell them what they saw and how they should live in order to have that connection," I asked.

Alejandro laughed and said, "The true seers, the mystics who had connected with the Earth and the cosmos didn't tell others how to live. They shared their insights and their visions with others and would encourage them to have their own experiences and visions. They would assist people by inspiring them, by telling them that the world and the universe are mysterious. They would encourage them to empty their minds so they could touch upon the mystery. To lose everything that they thought they knew so that they could become free in order to perceive in a fresh and untainted manner.

"An awakened seer resides in a state of presence. They come to know that true reality is only assembled and created when everything we think we know about the world and its workings has been released. This is why the practice of recapitulation is so important; it assists in the release of the many things that fill our minds and makes room for the energy of pure life-force energy to enter."

"So, seers of past and present," I asked, "are each connected to the oneness of Source and as such, they remember that they are part of the Lineage?"

"What they remember," Nayeli said, "is that they chose to manifest themselves into human form upon this magnificent Earth, and know why they chose to do so."

"Why, Nayeli, did they choose to be here?"

Alejandro suddenly laughed loudly. I had become so focused on all the energetic lines I saw in order to make sense of everything they were telling me, that his laugh startled me and jolted me firmly back to my chair.

I looked at Alejandro quizzically and he said to me, "Why do you think they chose to be here?"

Sitting in silence for a while, letting everything that I heard sink in, I glanced to where El Cuervo was lying in the hammock. Though his eyes were closed I couldn't tell if he had fallen asleep but was certain he was fully attentive.

"So that they could experience what it would be like to be in human form?" I said more as a question. I thought a little more and said, "Because they were existing as particles of pure conscious awareness in the cosmos and were able to perceive the diversity and beauty of the Earth. They wanted to manifest into form so that they could experience the grandeur of Earth through the use of their senses," I said with more conviction.

Everyone smiled, even El Cuervo, and I had this bizarre sense that the four of us were completely mad. As though reading my thoughts Nayeli said, "We are, of course, insane, for if we were sane we'd being living the lie like everyone else!" At that everyone, including me, laughed uproariously as if to punctuate the point.

I had been feeling extremely sensitive and raw since I returned from my quest. Nayeli and I returned to her home and settled in for the evening. As we sat restfully in her living room, I began to cry thinking with no comprehension on how it was possible for people to forget about our connection to the Lineage.

"What are the biggest luminescent fibers that people become attached to, Nayeli," I asked as I wiped my tears.

She answered without hesitation. "Fear is by far the biggest and shiniest line," she said. "One of the greatest things that people fear is old age. Just look at everyone out there getting plastic surgery and enhancements to fight the natural process of growing old. Fear of death is a big one too. Most people prefer not to deal with it and like to believe that they will somehow wind up immortal."

"Another thing that illuminates the energetic line of fear includes failure and everything associated with it like rejection, ridicule, and unworthiness. One of the biggest lies that has been imposed upon people for centuries is that they are unworthy and incomplete as human beings. The idea of unworthiness is a deceitful maneuver that was set in place by the system, the man-made matrix. It is insinuated from the moment people enter into this beautiful world that they are not whole. There are countless expectations to be met and adhered to through a lifetime of obedience and compliance. This, they are told, ensures their salvation and entry into the kingdom of heaven." She added with a heave of frustration, "Most people envision the after-life as some other worldly place that promises the amazing bounty and beauty that the Earth already offers."

"And then, upon the line of fear lies misery, poverty, and lack," she continued. "Within those fears are the additional fears of victimization and violence. People have forgotten how to exercise their freedom, how to stand up for themselves, and for what they believe in. They wind up remaining in bad relationships or toxic jobs, because they have become afraid of failing in something new. They would rather remain in the miserable states they are in than take a risk to improve their situation. Formal religion and politics has rendered people helpless by constantly telling them how unworthy they are."

"Then why don't people align with the Earth and Source energy, it's so simple," I exclaimed feeling simultaneously overwhelmed and exasperated. "It's right here on this glorious Earth. We are standing on it every single day of our lives, twenty-four hours a day, every day."

We were quiet for a long while, contemplating our own thoughts when a soft, warm breeze blew in through the open door to the veranda. Nayeli spoke, "The illusion of separation is prevalent in today's world. It is the cause for so much loneliness, depression, and disease, all fear-based factors. For far too long people have been told that they are simply bodies that have essential organs to keep them functioning and brains with which to make decisions and choices. By living only from their minds and not their hearts they have diminished their connection with the Earth and with Source energy. As a result they rob themselves of the energy, well-being, and joy that might allow them to live life fully.

"When people are ready, they will take the time to sit in silence upon the Earth. As they permit themselves the opportunity to experience a great shift of awareness, they will become more aligned with Source energy. The power of the Earth and Source energy of the cosmos are available to anyone who would want to connect with it. It is up to each individual to make that choice for themselves. They must be truly ready to make the commitment to become a warrior in order to cut through the illusory materiality that seems to rule the world. When their alignment with Source occurs, they will begin to recognize that much of their lives have been lived in a false state of separation from Source. But no one can tell them to do this, they must take responsibility and decide it for themselves. Until that time, they will only be able to continue to do what they know."

"And what is that, Nayeli?" I asked.

"They do the best they can with what they know while repeating and upholding the patterns," she replied.

We sat quietly for a while as I considered the truth of what Nayeli told me. Though afraid to ask, I did anyway. "What's the next brightest line, Nayeli?"

"Love," she answered, both surprising and reassuring me. I smiled.

A Dark Force

The act of being alive, of living and shaping our lives is an extraordinary act of creation. When we shape our awareness, we are freeing ourselves from the grasp and mindset of the dark forces of the earth, from the predator, that has become more powerful and more predominant than ever. It is not enough for a warrior to fight the predator by battling it to the end; one must remove themselves completely, remove it from their mind, and this takes patience, fortitude, and extreme courage.

- Alejandro

"Our challenge as warrior seers," Alejandro began, "lies in releasing the stories that have molded and shaped the ideas of what it means to be human. We must take an inventory of where the ideas of how we should live our lives came from, and then recapitulate those stories. When we undergo the process of release, we are able to assist others in becoming free from the historical grief they are experiencing. This helps them to reclaim their pure life-force energy which had become enmeshed and diluted within the ideas and patterns that were bestowed upon them and which do not even belong to them."

"So what you're saying, Alejandro," I said trying to pull together everything, "is that the committed warriors of freedom must continue to walk in alignment with the Earth and Source energy. This helps to keep the Lineage alive so that as many people as are interested may come to discover that their identities may not really be their identities after all. They may be merely echoing the patterns of a human collective that is often devoid of Spirit."

He and Nayeli nodded in agreement and Nayeli added, "People have been trained to fill specific roles of being human until one day they may come to recognize their lives as exactly that, the upholding of patterns, which is a foreign installation. When they are able to discern that their identities have been based on memories of the past and that they must be consciously sustained by means of constant self-reflection, they will have no choice but to begin to aspire towards something more. They will choose to stop comparing their existence to how others exist or through the reliving of the stories that have been told to them."

"So this foreign installation," I stated, "is like a program or an implant, something that has been embedded into human consciousness to keep people, among other things, fearful and compliant. It's a form of self-imposed mental slavery that disempowers them and ultimately produces unfulfilled, and sometimes destructive and dangerous beings. This must be the dark force that the wolves showed me."

"What wolves?" asked Nayeli. Alejandro looked at me, more like through me, and I knew that he was looking at my energy body. El Cuervo rolled out of the hammock and came over and sat on the ground near us.

"Well," I began as they each looked at me intently, "there were these four wolves that visited me. They frightened me considerably, but then I considered them as an omen. They delivered a powerful message to me."

I relayed everything that had happened on that frightful, stormy day and night and how I came to realize that humanity became separated from the natural flow of Source energy about 10,000 years ago. How there were people who were in control of everything and had made everyone dependent upon them for survival. How they domesticated animals and humans which has led to the state of barbaric despair in which we currently live. "It was a horrifying and deeply disturbing dark force."

Alejandro closed his eyes and sighed deeply. I came to know that when he did this he was drawing from the knowledge of silence which enabled him to speak with clarity and focused intent. "This dark force, or predator as it's been called," he began, "started like all things; as an idea. Someone long ago considered how much better it might be to settle into an area, cultivate food, and as a result reduce and eventually eliminate the need to hunt and gather. For a while this seemed like a wonderful solution to many people who spent their days leisurely tending to animals, caring for crops, then retreating to the safety of their dwellings each night.

"Over a short period of time, the community thrived and the population increased significantly. Some people began to venture out, to start their own communities in areas that were more abundant with prospective food sources. As this occurred, leadership positions were established, and those in charge did everything in their power to emulate the success of their previous community. More and more communities were built and they began to increase in size. To remain productive, tasks were allocated to specific people, people who would only receive food or shelter *if* they put in their allotted amount of time tending to their assigned tasks. Those who protested these subtle beginnings of slavery would leave to establish their own communities so they could function in harmony and balance, only to find that they began repeating the same patterns that they had learned from their previous community.

"What arose from this was a claim to land and a sense of possession, that people now had rights to the land and water and animals that comprised their settlements. They even grew to possess the people within the communities, forcing them into more laborious tasks while giving little in return. The people began to feel a sense of disconnection from the Earth, though in their confusion they probably did not identify it as such. They were unfulfilled and experienced anger, frustration, and loss.

"Fast forward to the wars. There were wars to protect their claims and to possess more. When outsiders came into the communities to take food, shelter, or laborers, the community defended itself by using the agricultural tools in their hands which ultimately led to the creation of weapons. This act marked the beginning of the arms race, a way to develop tools with increased power, range, and accuracy, a race that continues to this day."

I sat there stunned as I followed all of these frenetically charged lines that Alejandro was rapidly presenting from the past to the current moment. "Nothing has changed" I said quietly.

"No, nothing has changed," Nayeli said irritably. "Countries are pushing harder to have bigger, better tools of destruction. Greedy desires to possess more and more land along with every natural resource known to man continue to escalate. From here to the Moon and Mars and beyond, the

LORRAINE VOSS   179

drive for control and power over humanity has become the
conclusive agenda."

Exasperated, she continued. "This attitude has led to
horrible outcomes including slavery, mass production, overconsumption, and war, all to possess and control everything and
everyone. It doesn't even matter, anymore, what that possession
consists of. The illusory mindset maintained by the people who
aspire to accomplish global control has elevated them to preside
from the most prestigious positions. Sitting at the top of the
pyramid, weapons ready, they protect their prominence and the
material pleasures which they have amassed."

For some unknown reason my mind jumped to envision
kings and queens, global leaders, and politicians sitting before
the people with semi-automatics in their laps and I expressed
this to them with a chuckle.

"Don't be fooled," cautioned Nayeli. "The weapons that
they use are not so overt. They use weapons of manipulative
language too, designed to massage the collective unconscious
with both lies of praise and condemnation. All of this stems
from the first idea of so-called civilization, of having power and
control over the environment, animals, and people."

Everyone remained silent for a while then Alejandro said,
"Some say that this energy is otherworldly, that it has come as
an alien force to this planet. It is called by different names
including archons, inorganic beings, reptilians, and walk-ins."

"So are you saying that it may be extraterrestrial in origin;
that it came from somewhere in the universe to rule humans
and life on Earth?" I asked.

"No," he chuckled softly, "but that is what most people
want you to believe; so horrific is the predator that by assigning

it to some outer space origin, people avoid taking responsibility for it and place the blame outside of themselves.

"Haven't you ever wondered why there is so much finger pointing and blame in the world? No one takes responsibility for themselves or for much of anything anymore. The fault for nearly everything is almost always projected outwards and blamed on something outside of themselves, onto their spouses, their parents, their kids, neighbors, age, culture, characters on TV shows, the internet, politics, religion. Or the best excuse yet: because that's the way it's always been done. Maybe the devil did it or the dog did it, but by golly, it wasn't me. Do you see why it is so easy to even place the blame of corrupt systems of control on an alien force? By so doing, the culpability of responsibility for humans is set aside and their barbaric, vicious and cruel behaviors are easily justified.

"The predator," Alejandro continued, "is energy, not a being. Though working through humans on Earth, it is a predatory energy that over the course of thousands of years has had its lines enmeshed in everything: government, money, food, religion and spirituality, education, resources, and wilderness. It imposes itself upon us in every aspect of our lives by attempting to remove our decision making authority and has a hold over us in a subtle form of slavery. Slavery to an illusory world of man-made concepts that only serve to keep those who reside in a state of influence and power, lucrative and in control.

"Those who are appointed and elected into positions of power are given decision making authority. They convey rules, dictate rules, and uphold rules to ensure that the system is functioning with compliance and efficiency. They are often perceived as godheads, people who supposedly hold a modicum of integrity and wisdom and enough false superiority to warrant a palatial estate, sometimes with thrones, robes, scepters, and crowns. They are extremely pompous and self-important, however, they must ensure the upholding of the paradigm and like pawns on a chess board, they play out their roles with conviction for the sake of the masses.

"Now, once decision making authority is removed, people begin to lose the impetus to take responsibility for anything. They simply rely on being told what steps are necessary to follow because to do otherwise is counterproductive to the system. When the system feels threatened, it will seek retribution through retaliation by the devaluation of money and property. It has even gone as far as seizing the holdings of others. In spite of it all, humanity continues to spin, just as it did at the birth of civilization, around and around as unwitting slaves to a corrupt system of deceptive agendas rooted in greed and profit. Blinded to the schema through an outdated and corrupt reward system of unnecessary and obligatory consumption, those in compliance continue to run around aimlessly with the hope of receiving praise, rewards, and increased income. This payoff, no matter how slight, makes them feel worthy prompting more consumption, thereby keeping the wheels of this man-made machine well-oiled and lucrative.

"The predator energy has infiltrated the minds of humans and continues to confuse, dilute, transform, and nearly extinguish the Lineage, the natural flow of things. Life on Earth had been very fluid, everyone and everything moving with one pulse, one beat. Wildlife was plentiful, water was pure, and each person took what they needed without wasting anything. The predator has diluted the Lineage and has contaminated it with illusory concepts," Alejandro concluded.

Nayeli said, "the majority of the human population isn't even aware of the fact that they are prisoners to this system, this derivative of societal existence. The system has them believing that it functions in order to make life good for them. The system proposes that things like deforestation, mining, fracking, drilling, diversion, and control over every natural environment provides jobs for people so that they can consume more. The unattainable carrot has been dangled in front of them since civilization began. And the sad part is that most people are happy with the system and aspire to reach the carrot. Instead of preparing to go into battle against the predator, they arm themselves instead, for the battlefield of consumption.

"Our food," she continued, "is being poisoned, genetically modified and altered, pumped full of antibiotics and basically turned into intellectual property; just another thing that was once available as a gift from the Earth has become a possession for the system in control."

What I failed to understand is how the best and most natural things for people could become so easily corrupted.

As though reading my thoughts, Alejandro then explained that the goal of this system is complete uniformity of its citizens. "If the worldwide system succeeds in their cooperative endeavor to socialize and perhaps, one day, even impose a totalitarian world order, they will have accomplished the very thing that they set out to achieve."

"What is that, Alejandro?" I asked with a twinge of fear.

"A guaranteed food source for the predator. And they are well on their way with the implementation of their methodology while leading people into believing that they are still capable of choice. The predator is positioning itself to take possession of all things, including humanity and the Earth itself. In removing people's decision making authority, by imposing upon them man-made rules that are so far outside of the natural flow and order of things, they are taking away every aspect of freedom, vision, and creativity."

"I don't understand why people remain captive to this type of imprisonment; can't they see it for what it is? Aren't they aware of how maniacally manipulative and harmful it is? How do people become free of this predator? Is there some kind of revolution or uprising that will free them from it?" I asked as I grew more and more anxious.

"You must look the predator square in the face," said Alejandro. "You have to acknowledge that darkness exists in order to avoid becoming consumed by it. Understanding its existence does not mean that you become a part of it. It is an opportunity to examine it in order to know where it originated so you can understand its power and restrictions. Then you look away, letting the flow of Source energy serve as your guide."

I became deeply disturbed by all I learned throughout this conversation. I asked about the role of religion and what its place was in the scheme of things.

"Organized religion bears the mother lode of the predator energy through the propensity it has to worship false idols," Alejandro exclaimed. "By revering a false god that is neither Source energy nor the center of consciousness within ourselves, we wind up giving our power away. But such is the point with many organized religions; to distract you into believing you are not worthy and to ultimately smother the Spirit within, stripping you of your power as a creative force within the force of creation. The true essence of God as Source energy has become diluted and minimized within nearly all religions. While mystics attempted to convey the truths of the universe, those who seek to be in positions of control have weakened the truths with deceit. Instead of allowing for a universal power or energy of unlimited potential to exist within everyone, they created a god in their own image so that they could justify their agenda to oppress and control people.

"Salvation is one of the very bright lines of energy, constantly being fed as people pray for redemption. The problem with the man-made story of salvation is that it is not new. It has been cycling through time for centuries and is wrought with lies. I defer to the fact that organized religion is used as a tool to have power and control over people, to keep them rooted in ignorance. And as such, nearly all religion has been designed as a means of manipulating the masses into believing that a being that they worship is far greater than themselves. They are promised salvation, as long as they remain in compliance with the rules within their specific religion. If they question the leadership roles or motives of the god that they are instructed to worship, they are told that they will be punished and worse, damned to hell.

"Religion was designed for multiple reasons and dates back to the beginnings of civilization. The first of these reasons was to provide a substitute deity for the Earth from which people were being forced to separate. Temples were built and said to house the entity of Spirit, and those who governed the people from within these structures threatened people with messages of fear and punishment from wrathful gods. The thought was that if the powers that be could create a substitute deity then the Earth would eventually lose her powers of healing, nourishment, balance, harmony, connection, and unity: of independence.

"It was no secret during the dawn of civilization that human beings had the creative power to exist within constant states of creation and co-creation. By creating false idols that could presumably do everything for them, people relinquished their own power of creation and sacrificed being whole and regenerative beings. Over time when a person from within these new civilizations was to fall ill, instead of co-creating their own regeneration from Source energy combined with the natural healing plants from the Earth, they were diagnosed with illness and provided concoctions contrived by charlatans claiming to be experts in the field of cures.

"When threatened to turn over their own decision making authority for their very selves at the cellular level, they did so, no longer striving to maintain themselves as the renewable beings that they were. Their level of reliance on the system for food, well-being, and shelter increased significantly. These humans, who once existed in a state of gratitude and communion with the Earth and Source energy, now found themselves barely surviving in states of oppressed fear. Their ability to align with the energy of the Earth and Source energy had diminished greatly. The loss of decision making authority is the most tragic condition that the predator has imposed upon humanity.

"The predator subdues our Source-given creativity in order to disable us from being whole and regenerative beings," said Nayeli. "When we move from a state of fear and into love, our creative energies kick into gear and the form through which we are manifest can recreate itself wholly, from the cellular level. People have got to take responsibility for themselves by waking up and refusing to play the game! They must come to recognize that they do have the power to create their own dream, their own reality. To achieve this," Nayeli paused to inhale deeply, "and I am emphatic about this, they must reconnect with the Earth."

Alejandro stood up and stretched. He said that we had covered a lot of ground and were getting fatigued. I agreed. We walked back to the house and El Cuervo plugged his iPod into the speaker and put on some lively music that brought our spirits up. Alejandro emerged from the kitchen with a bottle of red wine, four glasses, and a box of chocolate. This was both a rarity and a pleasant surprise. Nayeli, El Cuervo, and I began dancing in the living room as Alejandro poured the wine. Before long we were laughing, having finally released ourselves from the somber mood caused by our day's intense and important conversation.

A New Era

Now that the New Age movement has completed its cycle, there will be an enormous surge of evolved warriors emerging. These warriors are the seers of a new era, an era that understands how to move fluidly through the portals to cross the bridge that unites Earth and Source energy.
- Nayeli

After a restful night's sleep, my mind still raced from all of the information that Alejandro and Nayeli provided. The scary part was that it all made so much sense. Even though countries of the world differed, and the systems in charge may be unique to particular geographic regions, it seemed that the entire world was being ushered into an standardized existence, a existence of homogenized neutrality.

Having returned to Alejandro's house after a shower and a quick breakfast, we found El Cuervo sitting in one of the Adirondack chairs and Alejandro on his tree stump drinking coffee. After greeting one another and looking at no one in particular El Cuervo said, "Every time human awareness is about to reach a tipping point, the predator ensures that humanity will remain a victim to the system."

"What do you mean?" I asked him a bit reluctant to start the morning's conversation with the predator. "And why are we starting off the day on such a sour note?"

"I did a lot of thinking last night," he responded, "about how Earth awareness is increasing. Take the New Age movement as an example. It was instrumental in breaking through social paradigms and religious dogma. Piggy-backing on the hippie movement, the New Age emphasized viewing the world, and even the universe, in a holistic manner. A strong emphasis was placed on acceptance and oneness. In addition, people's energy was redirected from conventional religion into learning about and reconnecting with the Earth as well as exploring deep states of meditation. The New Age opened up gateways into higher levels of consciousness."

I expressed my relief that the conversation had moved on from the predator; this new conversation was giving me more data to process.

"Before the New Age, the hippies realized," he continued, "that mainstream culture was flawed. They were driven towards a wide variety of spiritual beliefs. Some began to explore the diverse paths of Native American and Shamanic Spiritualties from North, Central, and South America. Some connected with Gaian and Neopaganism Earth-centered ideals that are eco-friendly and environmentally sound. Gnosticism and mysticism appealed to many people while some sought mind expanding consciousness through the use of plant medicines and psychedelics. Others started to experiment with eastern philosophies like Buddhism, Hinduism, meditation and yoga."

Alejandro commented that these explorations were all instrumental in paving the way towards awakening to the consciousness within. He added, "The hippie movement was considered a counter-culture movement and was rejected by conservatives, traditionalists, and fundamentalists for the simple fact that they were unable to perceive the world functioning in a design that was different from their own conventional and mainstream form of existence. The New Age movement, on the other hand, was embraced and accepted by a very large percentage of the population. The New Agers have succeeded tremendously in creating a culture where environmental and universal awareness results in holism and balance so that personal freedom can become rooted. This has set the tone for a new era to emerge that will foster an evolutionary process for achieving total freedom.

"The New Agers persevered so that people would recognize that they were capable of living from a place of individuality and self-expression through their connection with universal life-force energy. Doors opened and barricades came down. Holistic herbal remedies replaced prescription drugs, creative expression and artistry expanded into a more abstract realm, and inspirational music with expressions of nature sounds and harmonic melodies geared towards relaxation were introduced. There were many people doing fine work in alignment with true awareness. They were instrumental in placing attention on taking ecological responsibility as well as teaching people how to take on responsibility for themselves. They began to live holistically, encouraged to return to the natural rhythms of the Earth and the universe."

"A lot of great insight and knowledge resulted from this movement," I offered. I looked at Nayeli and asked her why the New Age movement seemed to have disappeared.

"As with all things," she responded, "there was a dark side. The downside of that movement was the lack of authenticity that arose. As with every movement, loads of people saw this as an opportunity to enter into this field and prey on the multitudes of seekers who were awakening or were interested in increasing their knowledge about the wide range of ideals that were being introduced and discussed. Many self-proclaimed gurus, so-called medicine men and women, and *plastic* shaman hit the scene with little knowledge, limited awareness, but loads of self-importance."

Alejandro then explained that even though people were beginning to take responsibility for themselves through a wide array of modalities that had become part of the new mainstream in society, the predator was quick to jump on the bandwagon of perpetual oppression. He explained how the explosion into a new and widely accepted diversion to the way things had been functioning for centuries caused an entire marketable industry of Spiritualism, self-help, psychic, and psychological therapies to emerge. While some of these products had integrity and nuggets of truth within them, there were more wolves in sheep's clothing than had been experienced in a long time.

So-called Gurus appeared everywhere, claiming to hold the keys to enlightenment while taking advantage of their adherents through money, control, and sex. Organizations surfaced offering certification courses in shamanism, allowing people to earn the title of shaman, without ever having walked the land. More often than not these people were accomplishing their certifications on an intellectual level and through textbook protocols instead of having actual experiences with the unknown. Through technological advancement, he explained, today one is able to accomplish shamanic training through online courses.

"Spiritual materialism hit an all-time high. People were

spending astronomical sums of money on all kinds of doo-dads and statues and crystals in addition to paying for knowledge and awareness that they could never receive from the dishonest people who were on the take," he concluded.

"That sounds awful. I don't understand how something so beautiful can be turned upside down so quickly!" I exclaimed.

"Oh, you have no idea," said Nayeli. "It was as though a council of predatory servants met in order to discuss and implement ways to distract and prevent the human race from actually experiencing any kind of positive, evolutionary growth."

I couldn't help but think how powerful the positive aspects of the New Age had been because of those who had readily made their knowledge and awareness available with integrity, humility, and real life experience. It seemed to me that those people were the true wisdom keepers, the ones who had a clear connecting link to Spirit, to the Earth, to the Lineage that Alejandro had explained to me earlier.

"Carlitos himself has been considered the godfather of the New Age," Nayeli added.

It was true, I recalled. Carlos Castaneda had indeed been one of the first to usher in the New Age movement. His first book, *The Teachings of Don Juan,* was published in 1968 and reminded people of the unlimited potential and unfathomable awareness that they have available to them when they connect with both the Earth and universal energies. As a result, many people came forward including Indigenous tribal elders around the world so that they could help, in their own way, to rekindle the flames of awareness that we each have within us so we can remember this imperative and essential connection.

"So what now?" I asked. "It seems as though the New Age

Movement and the Hippie Movement overlapped? Is there another movement that has begun that I'm missing?"

Alejandro laughed so hard that I became embarrassed wondering what kind of blunder I made. "At my age," he said, "the only movement I am interested in lies in my ability to stand up on my own two feet and keep moving." Everyone cracked up at that.

"Seriously though," said Alejandro still chuckling at his own joke, "we have already entered a new era. I don't know if you can call it a movement because it is not as obvious as movements in the past had been. What I see happening is that warriors have gainfully transitioned through the New Age movement by honing their awareness and attaining a profound understanding of the bridge that unites Earth and Source energy. They are recognizing that everything they need to learn at this point must come to them through inner silence. They have especially come to realize that there is just no substitute for personal experience and are committed to recognizing things and learning from their own perspective rather than being instructed or taught how to perceive."

We were quiet for a few moments then Nayeli said, "The energy of the earth has shifted as a result of the New Age. Do you remember how everyone was waiting for some apocalyptic or catastrophic event to occur in 2012? When it didn't, people seemed blasé about the whole thing, even let-down somehow. But when you look back at how many natural disasters occurred during the years surrounding 2012 you can come to the conclusion that the Earth was in fact shifting, shifting her awareness while simultaneously shifting the assemblage points of humanity. The shift was subtle but it was not lost on the warriors.

"Most everyone I know is going through or has gone though some major life circumstance that has challenged them to release the fixation of their assemblage points and access Source energy. Many warriors are recognizing it for what it is and can move through these challenges with fluidity. Some warriors are struggling a bit while the new conscious awareness takes time to settle in and become integrated and grounded."

"What about the people who are not warriors?" I asked. "Are they aware of this shift?"

"Many people are aware of it, though not all. Some remain completely oblivious to it. They continue to go through their lives in a monotonous manner while deeply anchored within the patterns of their lives. But it's okay, because as time goes on, the warriors of this new era will emit an energetic frequency, a vibration that will loosen the fixated assemblage points of those who are ready to emerge from their states of unconsciousness."

After a brief pause in the conversation, Nayeli continued. "The seers and warriors of this new era are working differently than before. One of the pitfalls of the New Age was that most people did not work together. Instead they worked alone, each competing with the other through the self-importance of having the only right or correct way to accomplish things. Many were still working to release the man-made patterns of dogma and struggled through that process. They lacked a unified commitment to each other, to each other's work. They formed secret societies and memberships, because they were unable to see how the strength of their teachings depended upon the whole. Instead, they worked ceaselessly, but alone.

"However," she continued quickly, "the people who were the true leaders of the New Age were deeply committed to the preservation of knowledge, conservation of the Earth, and the resuscitation of the Lineage. They allowed their knowledge to flow and felt honored to give it all away selflessly and freely. They knew that the strength of the whole depended upon the increasing knowledge of the whole and were willing to work together, in sync, in order to create a strong foundation for the knowledge they were imparting. As a result, you can say their work together assembled the bridge."

"What bridge is that, Nayeli?" I asked.

"The bridge that connects the Earth to the sky, to the Source energy of infinity," she replied. "The link that allows people to remember that there is no separation and that cooperation is key."

"Wow, that makes so much sense based on some of the experiences I have had with various New Agers over the years," I said.

"The warriors of this new era," Alejandro said, "recognize there is strength in numbers and because of that they are committed to shared successes. Each of them upholds great resolve and works diligently at deepening their connection to the Lineage knowing it is through this connection they will attain total freedom. They are able to see the cooperative intertwining of a system of energy as it flows through the universe. They have no attachments to the calculated strategies that come from those who aspire to achieve fame, influence or authority. In addition, they are beyond the inert practices of convention, obsolete rhetoric, and stereotypical tradition."

Nayeli's eyes were fiery, she seemed so enthusiastic about what Alejandro was communicating. "Yes, she said. "The warriors of this new era are doing what they love to do. They are passionately and creatively aligning with intent, awareness, and freedom so they may return, unfettered, to eternity. Often working in silence, they have become energetically united to tell a story of truth because of their commitment, because of their inherent bond to the Lineage. They have come to discover no one single person can do it alone. That no one person ever has and never will. They are dancing together along all of the lines of awareness, liberating whoever they meet by allowing them the very freedom of creation."

I began to see, to envision warriors around the world creating what I came to know as hubs of awareness. These hubs were formulated through the confluence of individual creative energy that form a nucleus of power through which the warriors are able to heighten their awareness and become energized. For most, the act of personal recapitulation had been completed providing them with ample energy, and they were collaboratively initiating a masterpiece of synergetic creation, re-creation, and co-creation on a dynamic energetic level.

Nayeli spun herself, as well as us, into an amazing and luminous web of energetic lines, each one vibrating and harmonizing in a dance of effervescent fibers. I saw the dull line from my quest now vibrant and oscillating with a magnificence that set it apart from all of the others. A sonorous sound began emanating from somewhere, surrounding us with its resonance. It seemed to move through us. I felt ecstatic and euphoric and could tell that everyone else did too. We were all connected. We were as one with the entire universe.

Evolution

Evolution begins with inner silence. Take time to sit in stillness and connect with intent to determine the course of action you will take in order to connect to the intricate web of which we are all a part. The light and humming of energy that vibrates throughout silence will immerse you profoundly into the pulse of the earth, into the rippling echo of the cosmos onwards to infinity.
- Nayeli

Nayeli encouraged me to talk to them about the third day of la búsqueda. I started by telling them about the antics of the hummingbirds, of the gigantic juniper tree, and how relieved I felt to be starting the day with warmth and sunshine. I related to them the feelings of oneness that I experienced, about connecting to the Earth through my root chakra and about the creative and balanced vibrations that I intuited and felt.

They were pleased to hear about a good beginning to my day, and I eagerly recounted how I witnessed people returning to the Earth to rekindle their connections to her. I told them about the contented workforce that I saw working with alternative energy solutions and of the happy communities of people that I witnessed. I shared, excitedly, how the animal populations were increasing and that people felt productive instead of depleted. I told them of the Earth programs that were introduced to the schools, and that everyone was healthier, happier and in balance with the Earth.

"This has to be true," I declared, "or why else would I have seen it? And if it is true then why are so many people still living within an outmoded paradigm?"

"Oh, it's true," said Alejandro, "but it's a slow process and one that will take time to fully implement."

"Why is it slow?" I asked impatiently. "It seems as though so many problems can be solved so easily. What is everyone waiting for?"

"These are not new ideas," he answered. "They are, however, sustainable ones that have the power to make people self-sufficient. It is never easy to turn a good idea into a reality. If it were easy, it would already be done."

"A lot of people are talking about the things that are necessary to evolve into a more sustainable existence," said El Cuervo, "but talk doesn't get you anywhere; you have to take action. Everyone has to become accountable for embracing the attitude that is required for cultivating innovation. To sit around talking about it or sporting bumper stickers for a cause without taking action does not contribute to bringing ideas into fruition."

"On the plus side," said Nayeli, "as creative solutions are being implemented, more and more people are beginning to explore their own creative possibilities striving towards new and evolved ideas of success."

"Yes," said Alejandro, "people are beginning to liberate themselves from the social order with great success. As supporters to the growth process of others, we have the privilege of bearing witness to their evolution. It is a joyful task as we have the honor of watching the true nature of another come into a state of remembrance of who they are and why they have chosen to be here.

"When people become empowered to live their own lives within the beauty and truth of their own beliefs they begin to become creative beings. This occurs because they have had the opportunity to bear witness to their own unfolding and blossoming as an act of creation within creation itself. For some, the realization of one's true nature takes time to integrate and identify with while for others, it is an epiphanic moment.

"So-called progress has taken 10,000 years to arrive at the state we are in, so it will take some time to release the old habitual patterns and an outdated paradigm in order to reemerge into a state of fluidity and creative vision. But forward movement is accelerating thanks to free thinkers, iconoclasts, visionaries, seers, and environmental conservationists who are not content to uphold a broken and damaged vision that brings so much harm to everything on this planet," Alejandro concluded.

"Nayeli," I said, thinking about her earlier response to me about the second brightest line of energy, "Please tell me about the energetic emanation of love."

She sat thoughtfully for a few minutes and I knew that she was gathering up many lines of energy through which to respond. She was beautiful to watch as she searched with her cosmic eye through all of the energy fields and opened herself to receive them into herself so that she could convey their vibration with clarity and precision. She took a deep breath and a smile appeared on her face. I knew that she had aligned with the nuggets of truth that lay within the lines of energy she had opened herself to.

"Love," she said, "is such an immense and beautiful thing. It has the capacity to completely permeate and infuse those who are open to being a conduit for it. When a person embodies love, they emit love, they are that very love. Real love is power; it is the power of the universe that flows, unencumbered, through all things. It is pure energy and does not take or demand energy from another.

"In loving the Earth with this level of intensity one can know what it means to truly love and be loved. It is a monumental surrender. When loving the Earth with unbending passion, all of Earth's inhabitants are loved equally. A seer loves all beings, all things equally and in utter freedom because they recognize them as creative expressions of Source energy. Loving in this way is an immersion, something that can be felt and understood but not explained. This level of love can be experienced when one is quiet, so quiet that they no longer exist. The Earth, as you have discovered, has a pulse, a heartbeat. If you take the time to connect to that pulse you will know in that moment that you are connected to everything. You will get a sense of what it means to love and be loved in utter freedom. Then you will know that you exist as a mere microcosm of all things simultaneously."

Nayeli's words had the power to envelop all of us within the beauty of her description and I could feel all of us vibrating intensely within the line of pure love. It was as though an electrical charge was running throughout each of us, connecting us together. I felt a tingling in my fingertips and the surface of my face. It felt as though all of my cells were dancing within me. I leaned back in my chair, closed my eyes and felt the flames of awareness expand within me. The beauty of the Earth cascaded before my eyes.

Nayeli sensed that we were all experiencing the embodiment of love and said, "Seers know how important it is to come from the heart at all times. There is a lot of fear in the world and the root of this fear comes from feeling unloved and of feeling unworthy of love. When people are given the opportunity to be loved and honored for their uniqueness and diversity, an amazing thing happens. They become comfortable in exercising their right to be exactly who they are, with authenticity and without fear. They begin to recognize that any restrictions or limitations to their own love comes from an age-old, false story of unworthiness. Then they start to release their limitations, and as they do, their own hearts burst open; love replaces fear, value replaces unworthiness, self-confidence replaces shame. When people are held in the highest regard, they are able to become the creative visionaries that they always were.

"What people have forgotten, however, is that love does not come from outside of themselves, it comes from within. There are people who spend their entire lifetime seeking love from outside of themselves, trying to fill a void with other beings or material things. Love, a feeling of intensity and depth, has become corrupted and turned into an external gratifying emotion. It is wrought with expectations and agendas instead of the deep sensation from within that you are experiencing right now. When we love and accept ourselves, we are able to hold all others in a state of pure and utter love with beauty, joy and freedom. Love ripples outwards, illuminating and freeing everyone in its path, a beautiful inoculation to age-old fears that have arisen from the false matrix that says: Love is yours, if..."

We sat in silence for a while, and I reflected on my own life. I have always felt deeply loved by others as well as having a large amount of the love for the Earth, the planet. Tinged with a deep sadness at times, the love that I know flows through me and exists as a force from within me. I looked at Nayeli and asked, "What do you mean when you say love has become corrupted?"

She closed her eyes, took a deep breath and said, "Sadly, most human beings were never taught to love, they were only taught right from wrong. While children are growing up they are taught to expect various responses as a result of their actions. If they do something that exists beyond the parameters of what is expected of them during their domestication, they risk facing negative, disapproving, and sometimes abusive responses. On the other hand, if they do something in accordance to the conventions of life as a human being, they receive praise, approval, and acceptance.

"What this has accomplished," she continued, "is a great diminishing of love for life, self-expression, vision, and individuality. Instead, children are taught at an early age to respond to gratifying emotions relevant only to themselves without much regard for others. They come to perceive parents, teachers, and other people as "the other" always keeping themselves on guard. This ensures that they react with the most appropriate responses to conversations and situations in order to gain approval regardless of how they may truly feel.

"People grow up without truly knowing love. What they are trained to do is respond appropriately, and that when they provide the expected responses, they are then worthy and lovable. They begin at an early age to live in a state of fear, the fear of not responding in the most appropriate manner. This causes them to forget that love is always there right inside of them, waiting to burst forth and clothe the world in beauty and in freedom.

"Romantic love has in many ways become the ultimate false truth. It has people falling over themselves in their ardent need to attain it. Rather than falling in love, people instead coerce love into occurring. The very idea of acquiring this kind of partnership has caused humanity even further separation from Source energy. This kind of love is based on desire, on wanting to possess another in order to fill the false hole and emptiness that we have been told exists within us. People wind up not seeking someone with whom to share love but rather to find someone who can live up to their idea of making them feel whole and complete. When the fantasy of their ideas of love begin to wane, these people are often reduced to things like neediness, co-dependency, neuroticism, jealousy, power plays, and even aggression. Just look at how conditional love has become, as though love itself were attainable as a thing to which other actions are measured.

"The simple feelings and states of pure love have turned into an intricate and complex concept from which many other emotional dysfunctions arise. Because of this, many people do not feel true love, and love itself becomes an empty concept that holds people prisoners within a perpetual state of unfulfillment.

"When people fall out of their states of so-called love they are often prone to divorce, depression, suicide, or violent crimes of passion. Can we then say that they were truly in love? No, they were experiencing the concept of love, the idea of love founded upon the conditions that were cultivated within them without any clue as to what unconditional love in freedom truly is."

"This sounds terrible, Nayeli. Why, if there are so many misunderstandings and negative traits associated with love, does the energetic emanation of it shine so brightly," I asked.

"Because as I mentioned earlier, the brightest lines are the lines into which people place a lot of energy. Even though they appear to be shiny and beautiful does not necessarily make them good. These lines are so obvious because of the fact that people give them a lot of energy. This makes them brighter as the result of the collective consciousness fueling them. On a subconscious level, people are attracted to them. Then their ideas of love are played out, and if their ideals are not met, this so-called love may become disastrous.

"The people who begin to manipulate and control each other are not living their lives in love. They are living their lives in compliance with the ideas that were implanted in them as children. They are playing out the patterns over and over again which more often than not lead to strife, despair and unworthiness.

"What sets seers apart from this type of love is that they don't feel love as a concept based on the thoughts and ideas in their heads; instead they feel love with their entire body as a result of constantly being fully immersed in it. This is accessible by being completely aligned with the Earth and Source energy. Allowing illusory things that serve as distractions to fade away into the background opens seers to the beauty of pure love that emerges from within themselves."

I became aware, during la búsqueda, that alignment with the Earth is not only a beautiful thing but a necessary and natural one. The Earth and I shared our pulse, our heartbeat, and an amazing, natural, and holistic ripple effect grounded itself in me. I awoke with all of my senses alert, knowing that I would, from this day forward, have no choice but to hear, see, smell, feel, and know the pulse of the Earth, to connect with it, to become one with it. In so doing I will be connected with silent knowledge, will be more attuned to myself, in sync with all beings, and aligned with Source.

Becoming aligned with this universal bond helped me to make sense of the things that Nayeli was explaining. For some, this universal bond is the great web of life connecting all things. For others it is the awareness of seeing all of the lines that intrinsically connect everything, each moment from here into infinity.

Only after my reflection did I speak. "So when we are in alignment with the energies of the Earth, we are able to know the totality of ourselves in alignment with universal life-force energy, able to know that we are part of creation as creator and created."

"Yes," said Nayeli. "Now do you understand why after doing the personal recapitulation it is so important to recapitulate the stories of the Earth?"

I nodded solemnly and Nayeli explained that the stories of the Earth prevent people from working as the creative entities that they were meant to be. Our lives were orchestrated and dictated for us, long before we were even born. Our parents and our grandparents and their parents before them upheld an unspoken and implicit agreement of conformity based on a monetary reward system. It became so ingrained it was nearly indistinguishable from the patterns of life itself on planet Earth. Like cogs in a wheel, the predatory energies of possession and consumption became the norm. Many people simply serve in the capacity that allows this grand illusion to be forever fueled and maintained without fail.

Alejandro, who I thought had fallen asleep in the hammock in which he rested earlier spoke: "As I said before, it is a slow process but people are awakening. They are becoming aware of the chains that bind them and are bored with the stories that they have been told. Seers, visionaries, and non-conformists are emerging in great numbers and are no longer content to serve an archaic paradigm that is motivated by money, power, and control. They are more gratified with restoring the Earth to her natural beauty and reconnecting with their own personal creativity, self-expression, and vision. They are aware that as individuals they are part of a greater whole. Though it will take time to fully alter the current paradigm, the shift is occurring right now."

Reconnecting to Feminine Energy

When female warriors enter silence with intention opening themselves to receive life-force energy, they become one with everything. It is in this moment that the assemblage point shifts significantly from its fixated location allowing access to the infinite. Female warriors, when impeccable with their energy, may guide others, with focused intention, through an amazing and powerful journey into the vast sea of awareness.
- Nayeli

A few days after the conversations with Alejandro, Nayeli, and El Cuervo, the skies opened up, and a deluge of rain poured down. I have always loved warm summer storms, especially when they include thunder and lightning. Nayeli and I were at her house canning the apricots that had grown profusely on her trees that summer. While I stirred the syrupy mixture of apricots, water, and sugar, we started to discuss the illusions that are upheld by the world. I asked her why the people of the world experience so much pain and suffering.

"Since our conversation with Alejandro the other day, I thought about how humans living life on Earth must seriously consider reconnecting with the feminine energy of the universe," she declared while removing the hot glass jars from the water bath canner with a pair of tongs.

We silently ladled the apricot preserves into the jars, and I let what Nayeli said sink in. "The predator energy truly is enmeshed in everything, isn't it Nayeli?" I asked. The conversations of the other day were still fresh in my mind.

"Oh yes, it certainly is. Many years ago," she said after wiping the rims of the jars, "I had been involved with a women's Spiritual group. Three of these women were very much a part of the New Age movement and had various certifications as healers, shaman, massage therapists, and the like. I silently referred to these three as the Woo Woo Mavens. A group of about ten women, including the Woo Woo Mavens, would meet once a month at alternate locations, and I would mostly listen as these women recounted their perceived inadequacies, woundings, shortcomings, and unfulfilled dreams. I would attempt to get these women to shift the position of their assemblage points by sharing empowering stories and had even spent an entire afternoon teaching them the practice of recapitulation. Some of them began to realize how trite and contrived their lives had become and recognized their potential to arrive at creative freedom. Then the worst thing you can imagine happened."

"What happened, Nayeli?" I asked eagerly, always interested in the stories she chose to share with me about her early days when she was very active with the outside world.

"One day I invited the women to my house for our monthly get together. As you know, I used to have a temazcal on my old property."

A temazcal is an adobe style dome structure of Mayan origin that was typically round and about four feet high with a doorway through which to enter. Similar to a sweat lodge, a temazcal has a pit in the center of it where hot rocks are placed.

When water is poured onto the rocks, a wonderfully cleansing and purifying steam fills the temazcal, which helps to purge toxins from the body. In addition, the temazcal serves as a gateway between the worlds, and is a special way to shift the assemblage point to bridge the Earth and universal energies.

"About a dozen women showed up with wonderful food to share for the pot-luck dinner that would follow the steam bath. For many of these women it was the first time that they had ever participated in this ancient ceremony. After everyone had entered the temazcal and we covered the door with a blanket, I began to drum the heartbeat of the Earth, a soothing rhythmic beat. After a while I explained to them about the pulse of the Earth while I steadily drummed. I knew that the mood had been set and as always, I invited everyone to offer up their gratitude for the Earth, the Spirit, and whatever else they wanted to give thanks for."

"It sounds lovely, Nayeli, I'd like to participate in a Temazcal sometime," I said.

She smiled and said, "After a while we brought more hot rocks in, and I began to shift their assemblage points by sharing a story with them about the wholeness through which they were born into this world and how all else is an illusionary chain of events. This was to encourage them to recapitulate the stories and events of their lives that they continue to cling to and even repeat. We started to go around the circle, each woman stating with clear intention the things that they were ready to release, This was done in order to reclaim and embrace the state of wholeness that they had almost come to view as irretrievable. There were tears and sighs and even anger expressed as they engaged in the process of release. A great burden was shed from the first three women as we progressed around the circle.

"One of the Woo Woo Mavens was next. She began by saying, 'While this is all well and good, a wound is a wound and cannot be denied. You cannot simply state an intention for it to be gone and expect that it will. In order to fully heal from the tragedies of your lives, you must consult with a certified healer to allow them to perform the work on you in which they have been trained. Without the kind of work that a professional has to offer, you can expect to remain broken and unhealed.'"

"Holy cow, Nayeli, what audacity!" I exclaimed. "What did you say to her?"

"First of all, you could've knocked me over with a feather. I sat in disbelief that she used this sacred space to promote her agenda. Once she completed her self-serving speech, I allowed the rest of the women to state their intentions. By now, the shift of energy that was created had dissipated due to her false and crude statement. A dark shadow of insecurity replaced the power of transformation. After the last woman spoke, I said, 'There are those who take responsibility for themselves and those who rely upon others to do the work for them. Unless you are committed to taking responsibility for yourself, you may very well remain enmeshed within the stories of wounding that prevent you from healing and positive growth.'"

"Wow, I can't believe you didn't call her out. Did you ever say anything to her about it?"

"No. Actually, I never spoke to her again. She most likely became embarrassed about her crude and inaccurate statement and stopped attending the circle. You see," she explained, "a person can never tell another person what they need to do or how they need to experience something. In so doing, they rob another of having the experience that they need to have in order to connect with Spirit in their own way. It is through their personal connection that they may have their unique healing or intuitive revelations. In addition, as long as someone continues to tell another that they are damaged, they will continue to believe that they are not whole and will impose that thought form upon others."

We began to remove the jars of preserves from the pot in which they had been processing for the past ten minutes. A few minutes after we had placed them on the countertop the jars began to pop, a sound I love indicating that the seal had been made.

"How could that woman, the Woo Woo Maven, be so mean?" I asked. "Didn't she realize the great gift that you were giving to those women?"

"You see, Nubecita, she wasn't what she claimed to be. She was functioning as something she was not, a wolf in sheep's clothing. She had a healing practice set up at her home where she received clients. Her livelihood depended upon doing her work for wounded people. If the women present reclaimed their power and accepted their wholeness, she would stand to lose clients.

"The predator energy is in everything, in the places you would least expect it. You just sometimes have to let it be. The women who were ready to walk into wholeness were able to do so and in so doing were also able to see how inauthentic and cruel the Woo Woo Maven truly was. And as such, they were able to rise above such nonsense and move on with their lives making an impact on other lives as they go. Sometimes it's not the people we touch, but the people who are touched by the people we touch."

"I don't understand how women have become so far removed from the natural flow of the universe, from the energies of wholeness and healing. I remember reading a book years ago about a woman who went to live with Aborigines of Australia. She recounted in her story the miracles of healing that occurred among these people. If they can heal so fully and naturally, we must all have access to that power."

"Of course we do, Lorraine, and it's not just women who have this power, it is the men as well. All beings of the universe have this power, but it was corrupted when civilization first began through the rise of false power. False power is the root cause of rivalry, opposition, separation, and an unfathomable state of hostility that, for whatever reason, has become prevalent throughout the world.

"Gnostics, mystics, and seers have made it known that the Earth, as nurturer, was a predominantly feminine energy. Once civilization began with all of its dualities, the feminine was perceived as ultra-powerful, even superior. Men wanted to be in control of everything, of nature itself, and religion became a very successful maneuver to diminish the power of the feminine by diverting power to the masculine in the form of a male god. As men lost their gentle and patient qualities, women were forced to become more aggressive as a means of self-preservation against this new male god that threatened to diminish their connection to the Earth. Balance with the Earth and others was dichotomized and thus began a sense of separation from the Earth and universal Source energy."

"So what can be done to remedy this state of despair?" I asked. "Something has got to change, people cannot go on living within such states of self-loathing and contempt."

"It is changing," she said. "The people of this world are coming together. They are uniting their energy. They are beginning to see themselves, once again, as part of a tribe, a really big tribe all working together for the good of the whole. The idea of having power over people or of holding all of the power is becoming a thing of the past. Unity will gain momentum and ripple out into the world.

"Each person has a special set of skills and talents that they are able to bring to the table to contribute to the greater whole. It is a creative and collaborative effort."

We were quiet for a few moments, and I envisioned this beautiful state of unification, a force of silent power as it began to energetically diffuse throughout the world.

"Will you be willing to undertake a task, Nubecita?" Nayeli asked.

"What kind of task?" I asked, uncertain as to what I should expect this time.

She laughed, sensing my uncertainty and said, "It's nothing big. I know how much you love the rain and how it inspires you. Would you be willing to go on a Spirit journey? I'll rattle for you while you hold the intention of people reuniting and reconnecting with feminine energy."

I thought that sounded like fun and told her that I would love to. She went to her room to get her peyote rattle. It was a beautiful rattle made from a small gourd, about two inches wide. She had attached the gourd to a handle made from the rib of a small saguaro cactus she had found decaying in the desert. She had painstakingly hand beaded a colorful, three inch long peyote-stitched geometric pattern at the top of the saguaro rib. Just above the beadwork, where the rib was inserted into the base of the gourd, she had tied seven small and unique bird feathers that she also found on the desert floor.

Nayeli collected little tiny shells on the beach to put inside of the rattle which gave its voice a delicate and otherworldly quality. We went outside together and she sat in a chair while I lay in the hammock, both of us protected within the covered patio.

Taking a few deep breaths, I closed my eyes. Nayeli began to rattle a very steady and rhythmic beat. It wasn't long before I began to drift fluidly into a state of dream. I could feel Nayeli's energy at the periphery of my awareness and realized that we were taking this journey together.

I asked silently, "Is it normal to reside in a paradigm where we must abide by rules that were established to provide each with a similar goal, a comparable life, an indistinguishable existence? Why is it that the majority of the population can no longer sense the power that lies at the center of their being?"

I had the slightest awareness of Nayeli nearby. I felt myself merging effortlessly into the universe as her rattle introduced its numerous voices. It carried me away, farther and farther, where immeasurable balance and harmony prevail.

A cloud began to materialize in my mind's eye. It was spiraling from the center and I caught a glimpse of Alejandro within it. He had a peaceful look on his face as he began to materialize into a serpent. A surreal quality permeated my being. I continued to watch him move through the clouds and when he emerged from one of them, someone was on his back. Looking closely, I saw that it was Nayeli. She looked at me, smiling, and then the serpent headed towards me. Nayeli extended her hand and I reached out and took it. A moment later I found myself sitting behind Nayeli on the serpent as it flew over and across the surface of the earth.

Before long the voice of Seeing entered my mind. "To look upon life as one of disaster, rejection, and failure merely represents acquiescence to what an old, man-made story of false power has predetermined. Personal gratification must come from within, from the very essence of ages past, where simplicity and flawlessness are firmly established. People must shed their disguise and return to the fluidity of Spirit while recognizing that all that has occurred is no more than a temporary obstacle hindering expansion. The path of the warrior is one of conquering, to triumph and stand strong in putting the past where it belongs, behind them."

The serpent that was Alejandro flew low to the ground and I dismounted. I watched as he, with Nayeli still on his back, flew up into the clouds and disappeared.

I was surrounded by a small gathering of men and women. We began to awaken to the smell of the moist, rich Earth, returning to a place of utmost familiarity. We were infused with remembrance of a time when we were one with the Earth. Within this state of being we were overcome with passion, and an abysmal sense of belonging, united in a place where we are serene and at home.

Savoring the moments of tranquility and warmly embracing the freedom that we experience in the moment, each one of us celebrates our ancient existence. We lose ourselves in the pulse of the Earth. We dance, uninhibited and graceful, with gratitude and appreciation for our lives.

With low sweeping movements of hands on Earth, the awareness of the absolute beauty and poise of feminine energy fills us. We are content and peaceful. The vibrant and gentle pulse of life-force energy moves through us, rekindles the flames within.

Many of us participate in the temazcal ceremony. We recognize the dark, moist, round space as a womb, a place through which to maintain and deepen our connection with Source energy in balance with the Earth. Emerging from the temazcal, we give thanks for the rebirth that we experience. Our minds are clear, our bodies pure, and our energy restored.

Aligning with the energies of the Earth, the seasons, the solstices and the equinoxes, we pay attention to the omens that present themselves. We recognize that everything happens for a reason. We move forward, ever mindful of our acts of creation and co-creation.

Deep gratitude for the Earth and all her beings, for Source energy and each other, allows us to know that our well-being is due to our interconnectedness to the true nature of life, no longer contingent upon external circumstances. Our souls expand and as they do, so does our state of awareness. The consciousness within us merges with all consciousness.

Reconnecting with feminine energy, we are able to unify and coalesce with masculine energy that had, for so long, been dominant. We know that the synthesis of feminine and masculine energies brings us to a state of equilibrium and symmetry that is energized with power, wisdom, and love.

A Warrior's Purpose

> *All we have to do is align with Source energy, merging with utter fluidity in the space of no-mind, no-words, no fixating, no need to explain. Just flow along as energy, witnessing energy, being energy, traveling through doorways and traversing the pathways that unfold before us.*
> *- El Cuervo*

Continuing to work diligently at integrating my experiences, I understood the complex machinations of humanity. Nayeli, Alejandro, El Cuervo, and I built a temazcal on Nayeli's property and were immersing ourselves with regularity in the emptiness of Spirit. We referred to the temazcal as our hub of awareness, and we shared that space with all who would come. Besides the physical purification that occurred as our bodies were cleansed with hot steam, we entered into the deepest levels of silence and began to access the silent wisdom of the universe. In it I discovered that there is so much more to life than we were taught to perceive. I had committed to eliminating the extraneous things from my life in order to become less dense in the material, as well as the physical aspect of my life.

I now understood why experiencing life while fully aligned and balanced between Earth and sky is essential to hone awareness. To venture out into the world offers us the opportunity to explore the Earth. We come to recognize acts of creation as they unfold. This provides us with knowledge, wisdom, and the potential to expand our own sense and style of creativity.

When we connect with the Earth or with silence, we are able to truly know what exists beyond our peripheral scope of being. This understanding allows us to surrender and open ourselves up to intent, to the source of universal life force energy, where we come to recognize ourselves as creators and co-creators. We simply cannot watch nature shows on television or read another person's claims and pretend to understand. Nature is deeper, much deeper than two dimensions. Without taking the time to have our own experiences, we miss out on the very nature of our being.

It was a beautiful day in early autumn. Nayeli and I drove out to the coast to walk along the beach and swim. I noticed, over the years that there were hardly any shells left on the beach. It made me sad because I always looked forward to bearing witness to all of the beautiful specimens that would wash up on the beach after each tidal exchange. The coastline of the Sea of Cortez is now crowded with homes. The beaches are scoured from dawn until sunset and every shell, stone, and piece of coral that washes up is taken by the beach combers. It is indicative of our society of mass consumption, taking and grasping everything within range and leaving nothing behind. I shuddered at the thought that one day, maybe soon, all of the living creatures on the Earth would be driven to extinction as the land they that live on, depend upon, is consumed.

After we walked about a mile, we sat down on the warm sand looking out across a vast expanse of blue-green water into nothingness. I asked Nayeli about the stories of the Earth, about our stories, the ones that make us think or feel that we are warriors. I felt her gazing at me and I glanced at her. Her eyes became narrow slits and then she popped them wide open and they were glistening. She laughed and said it is because we must find something to identify with, something to resonate with in order to feel as though we have purpose.

"Doesn't everyone have a purpose?" I asked.

"Everyone has a purpose, but not in the way that they think they do. People like to believe that they have a special purpose, a unique gift to share with the world. It provides them with a sense of importance. In addition, it allows them to feel as though their lives have meaning and that the world depends upon their ability to fulfill their purpose. People begin to dedicate their lives to what they perceive is their life's purpose so they can share and express their purpose to others. In the long run, this thought pattern has the tendency to create anxiety, doubt, and distress as people tie their self-worth to how their so-called purpose is received and accepted by others."

In the brief silence that followed I began thinking about my own inability in realizing what my life's purpose is. Never able to come up with anything significant, I felt as though there must be something wrong with me. It wasn't that I thought of myself as purposeless, more like a jack-of-all-purposes, master of none. I expressed these thoughts to Nayeli then asked her why I hadn't been able to find something to do in order to fulfill my life's purpose.

After a few moments she said, "Your purpose, Nubecita, has nothing to do with what you do."

I looked into her vacuous eyes and asked her what she meant.

"Your purpose Nubecita, just like everyone else's purpose, is to discover your authentic self and nurture who you are. It has nothing to do with what job you have or what goals you set for yourself. It is about coming to know yourself at the most profound level so at the end of each day you know that you are connected to the rest of the world through the simple act of just being."

"Oh Nayeli, you make everything seem so beautiful, simple and free."

"Life is far less serious than people make it out to be. There are so many expectations and instructions and guidelines and ideas that are undertaken and either upheld or released, depending on whether one is able to attain the particular outcome that they hope to achieve. It is important that we anchor our purpose within and give permission to others to do the same. When we externalize our purpose, we set ourselves up to become depleted of our energy. When we internalize our purpose, we find that we become increasingly energized, more joyful, more compassionate, and more connected to Source energy. Our authentic self begins to glow and effervesce.

"You begin to remember where you came from and to where you will return. You have undergone an amazing appointment with power through la búsqueda de silencio. Through your journey you were able to observe and perceive things far beyond what is experienced by most. Even though some time has passed since your quest, you will find opportunities arise that will trigger something else that was presented to you. In the process of your experience, you are able to more fully know who you are and what it means to be a creative human being within the universal flow of energy. That is your purpose, everybody's purpose, to connect with the universal life-force energy and become one within the eternal flow."

Just like a fractal, I mused. An infinite fractal of the universe flowing into infinity, not with an individual purpose but within the natural flow of all things.

"Thank you, Nayeli," I said as I got up and started to dance and twirl on the sand. I felt freer than ever and ran into the sea and back onto the sand, overdramatizing my dance of joy by raising my arms high into the air and tossing my head to a rhythm that was coming to me through the top of my head and the souls of my feet. I even did a spontaneous cartwheel which elicited a loud laugh from Nayeli.

"Oh Nayeli, how is it that life is really so simple and people make it so difficult," I asked sitting down next to her again, taking a drink of water from my water bottle.

"Every person on Earth has a myth with which they are aligned. For most, their myth belongs to another. They seek out the myth that best defines the patterns of identity that they would like to be associated with and then they put their house in order, so to speak. For some it is to look and act like those who they may consider a role model for them. For others, it is to attain positions of authority and power. They choose these roles in order to be accepted or to have control, without ever once considering their ability to use their own powers of creativity."

"A warrior, on the other hand, designs herself. She sees herself as a blank canvas and becomes open to the possibilities that exist in which to create her individual and unique manifestation of form in this world. She is prone to explore all possibilities, and while she dances along the lines of awareness that are already upheld by mainstream society, she remembers that there are always new energetic lines to discover and to create. She comes to understand that reality exists before birth and after death and that the details are illusory while we walk upon this Earth."

"I like to believe that I have been dancing along the lines of awareness, Nayeli, that I have recapitulated enough to gain the energy necessary for creating my reality. I don't want to depend upon the stories and visions of others."

"From my perspective," she said, "you have accomplished your task of recapitulating the stories of the Earth. You have heard and seen her stories and you are dancing along all of those lines of awareness without becoming attached to any of them. You and El Cuervo both came to understand the origination point of the stories and successfully recapitulated them at their source, together and individually. By so doing, the mythologies of those stories fell away effortlessly. As a result you restored your universal life-force essence and have the necessary energy to align with the assemblage point of the Earth.

"You have come to understand this physical plane, its beauty as well as its evil. As you demonstrated so beautifully a little while ago, you are learning how to dance in carefree abandon with the higher energies, allowing the luminous fibers of your being to connect with the unknown and transport you beyond time and space.

"As more and more people take the time to access the awareness that something more exists beyond the material distractions and bombardment of confusing thought patterns, they will begin to create themselves into extraordinary beings. Those who don't only know that they must grab onto what they are capable of aligning with in their limited knowledge. The position of their assemblage point becomes fixated and works to repeatedly justify and solidify that position of their ego."

"Please explain the luminous fibers to me, Nayeli," I asked.

"You saw them in la búsqueda de silencio. All of those lines of energy are the luminous fibers that exist and flow throughout the entire universe. Emanating from each person are luminous fibers. Those whose assemblage points are fixated on one or two specific modes of being emit very few lines, just enough to connect them to the lines of awareness with which they desire to be connected."

"Can you see my luminous fibers?"

"Yes. You emit a great quantity of luminous fibers. Since your assemblage point is no longer fixated, your luminous fibers move with fluidity. When I look at your energy body, I am reminded of beautiful and delicate soft sea corals, flowing gracefully with the surge and currents of the sea, each fiber moving of its own volition in freedom from the constraints of conformity and rigidity. Like the coral, you have little feelers moving out in all directions, providing you with the opportunity to connect to multiple lines of awareness simultaneously. The challenge for you now is to release your attachment to the lines that bring familiarity. This will help you come to know how ephemeral your life in form upon this Earth truly is."

I began to panic, unclear about what Nayeli was trying to tell me. "I'm so afraid that if I release my attachment to the familiar that I will have nothing left to hold on to. Will I float lost and aimless throughout the cosmos as my empty shell of form continues to go through the motions upon the Earth?"

Nayeli smiled at me, a warm, sincere and compassionate smile. "You will not be lost or aimless, Lorraine. You will be purposefully aligned with the flow of intent, with Source energy, as you move more deeply into the mystery of the unknown. This is what you have been preparing to do for many years; to be able to move within this world touching everything sparingly without leaving a trace. You are la guerrera, a female warrior, who has worked diligently to remember who you are, where you came from and how to connect to the power of the universe. You have connected to the void within and are now free to explore the void of the infinity."

There were tears in my eyes. "Oh Nayeli," I wept. "I am so incredibly grateful to you for everything you have given to me. If it were not for you I would probably be repeating the patterns of humanity, caught in the endless cycle of repetition. Thank you so much for everything you have shown me."

Nayeli stood up and reaching for my hands pulled me up so I stood on my feet facing her. She said gently and humbly, "I have not shown you anything. I have simply held the mirror in front of you so that you could see the incredible image of who you are reflected back to you."

I hugged her fiercely, feeling both melancholy and exhilarated. We walked back the way we came, along the shoreline when I looked down and saw, for the first time in many, many years, a beautiful, intact, tiny sand dollar. "Look Nayeli, I think I found the last sand dollar!"

We both laughed, but deep inside we were each profoundly sad at the thought that this may one day be the reality.

Earth - The Final Recapitulation

You do not undergo your final recapitulation so that you may forget this amazing Earth. You undergo your final recapitulation so you can enter total freedom as the Earth, in pure awareness and ultimate unity.
- Nayeli

The last thing that Nayeli said to me the day that we found the sand dollar on the beach shook me to the core.

We returned to the house with some fresh shrimp that we bought at the coast and prepared for dinner. When we finished eating we sat on the veranda. The evening was cool and stars were beginning to appear. We were both looking up and saw a shooting star with an extra-long tail sailing through the sky until it burnt itself out. Nayeli said, "that was the omen I have been waiting for."

She paused for a while as if collecting her thoughts and said, "I know how much you love this Earth and all of her beings. I am aware of how sad it makes you to witness the unnecessary destruction that occurs and escalates daily."

We sat in silence for a few moments. She seemed to want to say more and was looking for the right words. "It is time for you to take on another task, one that will provide you with the energy necessary to make your final journey."

I looked at her expectantly and a little fearful because she was in such a somber mood and not her usual vivacious self.

"The time has come for you to recapitulate the Earth."

I audibly gasped and could feel my heart rate increase. "No! I can't. I won't!" I began to weep and it quickly turned into deep, heart-wrenching sobs. I knew she was serious.

She got up and came over to stand behind me. Putting her hands on my shoulders she said, "I know how deep your love is for this Earth and you think of her as a mother to all of life. But you must remember that recapitulation doesn't mean denial of her, it is just a way for you to further clean your links so your attachment to her may diminish. This will allow you to be free from her and she, free from your attachment to her."

"I never thought of it that way," I said through my sniffles allowing what she just said to penetrate. But the immensity of what she asked hit me hard, and I started keening in loud wracking sobs at the thought of releasing the Earth.

With her hands still on my shoulders she said, "Don't be sad. You are going to come to see that this is a beautiful undertaking. You are going to accomplish the most magical of all things. You are going to merge your energies with the Earth and with all of life upon her. You will unite with her awareness and become one with her. This very act will allow you to pulse in sync with her, with the universe, with all of existence."

"Have you done this Nayeli, recapitulated the Earth?" I asked.

"Yes," she answered as she returned to her chair. "And as a result I have come to realize that when we recapitulate the Earth, we unite with the awareness of the Earth and recognize her for what she truly is."

"And what is that?" I asked eagerly.

"The Earth is not our mother, she is our sister."

My entire being seemed to tingle at this statement. I felt light and dizzy and giddy and curious and although this was something I had never considered before, I knew deep within my heart that it was true. I remembered something and I knew it was important. My heart felt as though it were about to explode with gratitude, love, and compassion for this beautiful sister Earth of mine.

"Powerful, isn't it?" asked Nayeli. "It's amazing how one simple word can change the entire context of meaning."

"I can feel it, Nayeli. I can feel it to the core of my being. Please tell me more," I implored enthusiastically.

"Our sister Earth began her journey as a spec of pure conscious awareness in the universe, just as you and I did. Just like everyone and every creature upon this planet did. She is an ancient, sacred being birthed of unconditional love and compassion. She is the origination point of this divine, Earthly Lineage, the mother of invention. In the same way that all of life began, she flowed in freedom through the cosmos anticipating how to manifest her awareness into form."

"She witnessed other forms emerge for eons throughout multiple solar systems and was familiar with that which manifested as stars, moons, suns, and planets. She observed meteors, comets, and asteroids and was familiar with all of the elements and forms that she came to know throughout the cosmos; fire, ether, water, light, darkness, and stone. Through these she knew heat, cold, ice, hardness, and softness. She decided she would create a mighty creation, one that could host a multitude of awareness in whatever form it so desired to manifest."

"She has existed in her creation as a self-sustaining planet for four point five billion years allowing for whatever changes need to occur. She consistently provides nurturing and nourishment for all who arrive. Seasons come and go; forms came and go; animals, plants, and bacteria came and go. All of these have been and continue to be acts of co-creation and manifestations of awareness from the cosmos in billions of different forms and species, a continual array of evolutionary creation."

"Where do the ones that became extinct go?" I asked.

"They return to the cosmos to integrate their new awareness and either manifest themselves elsewhere or in different form. Some choose nothingness. One day around six million years ago, a point of awareness in the cosmos chose to manifest itself into a creature that could walk on two legs. Seeing how brilliant that seemed, another point of awareness chose to do the same, and then another and another. Through the process of evolution, fine-tuning, and a myriad of adjustments, modifications, and alterations we arrive to the present time of human beingness."

She explained to me how, over time, those points of awareness throughout the universe that had manifested into form forgot that they had done so in order to experience the beauty of life on this amazing sister. They forgot that their time here was a transitory and ephemeral part of their creation. They became trapped within a rudimentary two-dimensional misrepresentation of their full-potential as creator beings.

"They like the illusion of life so much," she continued, "that they keep coming back, over and over again. This is what has become known as the karmic cycle of death and rebirth.

They no longer exist in fluidity and oneness as creative expressions of Spirit. Their attachment to form has solidified, instead, through continuity of identity on the level of form. To uphold form requires the conscious act of relying on memory, which is why so many stories and patterns continue to be upheld. This thought process created the myth of separation from Source and with it, the fear of being alone.

"This is precisely why the practice of recapitulation is so utterly important, to be able to have the memories without being energetically attached to them. We must never forget our ability to be free or we will remain enmeshed within the karmic cycle of repetition."

Nayeli thoroughly succeeded in shifting my assemblage point. No longer sitting on the chair next to her; I found myself floating through the cosmos, a witness to all acts of creation. I merged with the beauty and the magic that is devoid of self-identification. I sensed my deep and total connection to everything through the emanations that emerged from my own form. This allowed me to unite with the emanations of the universe and with all things in existence as well as those that were not, as yet.

The world as I know it dissolved. Even subtle sounds merged completely with the sound of the one, the primordial sound from which the entire universe evolves. The sound that embodies all sound surrounds me, is in me, is me. I recognize the sound. I remember it from before I took form. It is the sound of the infinite, the sound without beginning and without end. It embraces all that exists.

My consciousness flows through infinity. Infinity is nothingness. I realize that I'm not anywhere, and yet, I am everywhere. I know that I am everywhere because my mind is dormant and every cell in my body perceives my connection with everything. Everything disappears into the deep sea of awareness only to appear again.

I cling to nothing, no thoughts, no memories, no opinions or emotions. There are no illusions, attachments, dualities, or concepts. The only thing that exists is my ability to perceive creation from pure consciousness. I am provided with the ultimate opportunity to remember and connect to the awareness that separation and death do not exist. There is only oneness and it is empty; devoid of everything except the potential to create. It is consciousness that holds awareness in these moments, not me.

As energetic lines flow and connect and link all of universal creation in a powerful web of form and emptiness, pure consciousness reminds me that as long as consciousness exists we are eternal, infinite, and free. This remembering propels me through emptiness as more and more universal potential and creation reveals itself. Perceiving the creations of conscious awareness is vast and unlimited. Everything functions within the universal flow of energy on the waves of infinity without resistance. Realities, galaxies, star clusters, black holes, and nebulae dance without restraint.

I would like to express that I am ecstatic or blissful or joyful but the fact is, there is only nothingness. Neither good nor bad, it just is. Flawless within its perfection.

My human senses begin to materialize, once again, as my physical form and the world around me begin to reconstruct. I have forgotten where I am. I open my eyes to find myself looking at Nayeli. Everything is so impeccably complete and whole within the chaotic, yet organized layers of awareness that embody my sense of reality, or maybe my illusion, upon the Earth. I close my eyes again and take a deep breath. I accept the essence of Source energy as the center of consciousness within me. I murmur a hushed thank you as I exhale.

I had lost my identity and could not be happier. I understand why we are warriors, battling each day to avoid the demise of living our lives in fear and without luster. We choose, instead, to be creators: to gather experiences in awareness and in alignment with our original intention.

Very gently Nayeli said, "Do you now understand why we must continue to magnify and reflect the beauty of life on Earth to all who seek to flourish as a result of seeing that wonderful reflection? To remind these Spirit beings who are trapped within form to gently awaken so that they may come to remember they are free, have always been free, and must shed the illusions that keep them bound in form."

"Yes," I whispered. "I understand."

"Your challenge now is to awaken from the relentless lure of matter by recapitulating the Earth. As you recapitulate the Earth you are, in essence, recapitulating the vision and creation of your sister, the Earth. With appreciation and love, you will give her your gratitude for every single life form that is, ever will be, and has ever been in existence upon her. In so doing you will be honoring her and setting her free. In return she will set you free by providing you with the final energetic boost that is necessary for your return to infinity. It is from infinity that you may choose to create or recreate yourself in freedom and with awareness."

My recapitulation of the Earth took many years, following that conversation with Nayeli, and it was rigorous. I traveled from one geographic region to another delighting in the splendor of constant humility, appreciation and gratitude. Sometimes I traveled with El Cuervo, sometimes alone. I sat by rivers, breathing in everything I knew about rivers, their coolness, their sounds as they ran over rocks, the fish and insects that lived within them and the plants that grew at their banks. I recalled my own delight in splashing in rivers and collecting shiny, smooth stones from within them. My recapitulation of rivers led to a profound connection with them, ever expanding and freeing me further.

I recapitulated the forests, the smell of the damp soil, the ferns and the boulders, the trees and the moss, the mosquitos and deer and all of the sounds and tactile experiences I had while within them. As I walked through the forests I saw many stately creatures; moose, bears, wolves and grouse, squirrels and chipmunks. I gave gratitude to these for their own creative manifestation into form and released the playful otters, the graceful heron and the majestic eagles, hawks and ravens flying overhead. Sitting at the top of cliffs and looking out over craggy mountaintops and rolling hills, I released it all while simultaneously feeling as one with all of it, was in fact, all of it.

Traveling to the sea I recapitulated the sand and the shells, the dolphins, the whales, the sharks and the coral reefs. The way that I felt so buoyant while scuba diving, releasing the surge, the tides, the waves. Gaining more and more energy throughout what turned into the most beautiful moments in my life, I remembered the tiniest creatures, knowing that they were my brothers and my sisters, united forever in the great sea of awareness.

At the edge of a large and murky pond I recapitulated the snakes, the turtles, the alligators, the amphibians and the dragonflies and hummingbirds. I released the seasons, the cleansing rains, the fog, the mist, the snow and ice, the heat and the cold. I thanked the winds for all of its powerful lessons and released the wheel of life.

Each moment of recapitulation brought me more and more energy. I breathed the life-force energy deep into my womb, feeling the energy of the forms I recapitulated fill my entire body with awareness; merging and uniting with everything. Then, exhaling from my womb, I released all of the energy, letting go of any attachment to those forms.

Every release provided me with the energy to see and know more of Earth's creatures and plant beings. I recapitulated the insects and the algae, the melting glaciers, the geysers, and the waterfalls. I recapitulated the soil itself.

Through this massive undertaking I came to know my unity with all living things on the Earth. They were my kin, my equals from the same Source on a journey of discovery and of life. I knew beyond the shadow of a doubt that what happened to one thing in this fragile web of life happened to all things within the web. With great compassion, I earnestly hoped with the totality of my being, that the Earth and her beings would one day come back into balance.

As pure conscious awareness I could perceive and observe everything on the earth that I had recapitulated. There, before me, was a beautiful and diverse array of creation. The world, I realized, will go on with or without me. The patterns and man-made stories of the world will continue, only as long as there are people who are willing to uphold them.

My heart was full, my mind was free. The deep and endearing love that I felt for my Earth sister and for all creatures expanded beyond what I ever thought possible. I came to truly know power as it moves through the universe. With perseverance and resolve I released all attachment that I had to both collective and personal human knowledge to include all human structured concepts, mythologies, beliefs, and traditions.

Basking in a state of pure perception, I relaxed, appreciating my return to becoming awareness.

Made in the USA
Middletown, DE
30 January 2017